TEAM
MASTERY

TEAM MASTERY

From Good to Great Agile Teamwork

by Geoff Watts

First Edition Published 2020 by Inspect & Adapt Ltd
96 Redgrove Park, Cheltenham, Glos, GL51 6QZ

ISBN 978-1-9164394-5-0

Published March 2020

Edited by Ultimate Proof Ltd
Cover Design by Ole Størksen
Illustrations by Ole Størksen
Interior design by Frode Karlsen

Dedicated to

Grayson.

Against all odds,
sometimes miracles do happen.

Table of Contents

Index of Milestone Cards

Self-Improvement

Quality

Unity

Audacity

Delivery

Foreword by
Lyssa Adkins

Congratulations! You are the proud owner of an effective and fun way to help your team step into the empowerment that agile "gives" you. This book is a treasure trove of insightful and enlivening ways for your team to improve itself. But, wait… don't teams need people to show the way, like ScrumMasters/agile coaches? Team leads? Sure, especially at first, when your team encounters this whole new way of working and needs a good start, or when things are really off the rails.

I have spent the better part of ten years equipping those doing agile coaching (ScrumMasters, agile coaches, agile managers) to help teams undertake the arduous/joyous trip into the agile way of working and being. My premise was simple, perhaps naively simple: once those doing agile coaching mastered the 21st century leadership skills needed to flourish in this brave new world, those skills would naturally transfer to the teams. I assumed that we would see teams push back on unrealistic expectations, we would see delivery of quality products that matter, we would see high-quality team conversations that produce something truly novel. In short, we would see teams drastically increase their competence for creativity, conflict, and collaboration, to name a few.

For myriad reasons, despite all of the great work that those in the agile coaching profession have done, this premise of building team capability and unleashing genuine empowerment has not come to pass on a large enough scale to significantly increase the health of the worldwide practice of agile. There's a gap, a hole. I believe this book for team members is an important part of filling that gap.

The team you are on can do a lot of things for itself, if given a roadmap and compass to guide the path. This book is that roadmap and compass. It doesn't tell you about everything you and your team-mates will encounter on the trip, and it doesn't nullify the need for agile experts, coaches or leads. What it does is activate your team toward its own skill building. It points a direction, gives road signs along the way and offers needed rest stops where the team members can pause, look around, enjoy the view and say, "Hey, we did that!"

Those accomplishments are vividly described in Geoff's book, so that team members know when they have arrived at a new level of capability on their journey to mastery. When they do, there is a tear-out card they can use to acknowledge, celebrate and lock-in their new skill.

One of the things I enjoy about this book is that Geoff enacts key professional coaching skills in the way the book is constructed. Through relatable stories, he normalises the most common mindset and habit shifts experienced by highly capable agile teams. The skill of normalising reassures: "Yes, it's common to feel a bit vulnerable as you build this capability. If you're experiencing that, you are normal!"

So often, the agile way of working has people feel like a fish out of water. They don't know that it's normal to feel exposed and even gasping for air sometimes. If they know it's normal, expected, and won't last forever, they have powerful information that helps them build the capability faster.

The other professional coaching skill that shines through in this book is championing. Geoff lays out the key shifts a team can make to become healthier, happier and more productive. He entices teams to keep going through the use of his SQUAD model, setting up each new possible advancement. I can almost hear him saying, "Yes! This shift! Come over here, and see if you can do this one, too! I know you can."

I'm with Geoff. I say, "Come over here! Use this book well and enjoy the ride. You can make this shift. I know you can!"

Lyssa Adkins
Agile & Leadership Coach
Author Coaching Agile Teams

Foreword by
Andrea Tomasini

Geoff did it again. He has managed to build a whole book and a lot of very educational and relatable stories around an acronym: SQUAD!

Without spoiling it, I can tell you that each letter is worth reflecting on and letting it change you from within. Remember, the only person we can change is the one we see in the mirror every day... and, by changing ourselves, we can inspire others to do so as well.

This book is a great inspiration. Geoff engages us with stories we can all relate to. I often found myself saying, "Oh! That's exactly what happened to us as well..." But it's not just narrative; Geoff also explains the rationale behind why those situations happened and offers you a couple of possible ways you may solve similar issues within your own team.

Perhaps one of Geoff's greatest abilities is that he can explain even very complicated things with clear examples and without resorting to telling you what to do. His coaching stance comes across throughout and he does not try to tell you what is right or wrong. He shares the ideas and approaches that the teams he has worked with have used successfully and exposes behaviours, disciplines, attitudes and psychological aspects related to working as individuals and as a team, which make you reflect deeply.

This is a book I recommend you always keep to hand, and read over and over again, because I am pretty sure, as your experience and maturity within the team grows, you will find aspects that you didn't fully understand the first time. Given the many suggestions and tools that Geoff presents, there will be opportunities to pick up this book again, and each time the need will emerge.

Geoff's idea of including cards is great and I feel compelled to apply those techniques, tools, or new approaches and prove that I am worthy of tearing off another one of those cards! Although these milestones aren't about doing or making things once. Perfection is just a moment in time, in a specific context, and when we have experienced that once... we can't let it be, we need more, because it is satisfying. It is enjoyable and challenging to best yourself over and over again!

Thanks Geoff, for sharing such wisdom and experience with an impeccable coaching attitude, championing and challenging, while supporting and encouraging your readers.

Andrea Tomasini
Agile Coach, agile42 GmbH

Introduction

This book has been too long in the making. In my other books, I focused on specific individual roles such as the Product Owner, the ScrumMaster and the coach; and I have been delighted to hear so many personal stories of how those books have helped people become better in their roles.

All of the roles I've written about have one thing in common. They exist to serve – or get the best from – a team. Today's complex and fast-changing world needs cross-functional and self-organising teams to deliver value at speed while maintaining high quality. Teams are the key unit of value-delivery within today's organisations, where the difference between product success and failure is often more dependent upon the engagement of the team than even the quality of the idea.

A great idea will not be successful if it cannot reach the market in time at a high-enough level of quality. A great idea will not survive if it cannot be iterated upon based on the rapid feedback from its users. And the main factor behind whether an idea gets done well, quickly and responsively is the team.

As with my other books *Scrum Mastery* and *Product Mastery,* this book takes experiences from real teams and highlights what separates the great teams from the good ones. I share stories that will likely resonate with your own experiences of being part of a team and some that will inspire you to try different things to reach new heights of *Team Mastery*.

Being part of a great team is an almost magical feeling. I often ask people about the highlights of their working career and, while individual achievements do get mentioned, more often than not people talk about a time when they were part of a great team.

One of the first questions I ask the teams I work with is, "What kind of team do you want to be?" I do get some quizzical looks when I ask this, but the answer tells me – and more importantly the team members themselves – a lot about the journey ahead of them.

At its most basic, when given the choice between being part of a great team or being part of a mediocre team, almost everyone that I speak to chooses the "great" option. They don't always believe it is possible, but that's another question. The important thing is to capture the desire to be great, because then we can define what "great" means for them.

Although each team has their own definition of greatness – after all, every team is unique – over the years I have found a significant overlap in the hundreds of definitions of Team Mastery that teams create.

And that is why I have created this book – to distil those common factors of greatness from the many self-organising, cross-functional teams I have had the good fortune to observe and work with.

Team Mastery Takes Time and Patience

It isn't enough to get a group of people together and tell them to act as a team. Even with the best of intentions, teamwork takes time to establish. Plenty of models exist that explain the journey most teams take, from Tuckman's Stages of Team Development [1] to Lencioni's Five Dysfunctions of a Team [2].

I think these models are helpful as general guides, but the way individual teams develop is unique and depends on many factors, including their specific context and the personalities in the team. That's why I do not describe a model or a journey that all teams will go on.

Instead, I identify five characteristics common to all great teams: Self-improvement, Quality, Unity, Audacity, and Delivery (SQUAD). I supplement these characteristics with milestone cards, which are significant events in a team's growth towards Team Mastery and should be celebrated whenever they are reached – either through conscious effort or as a result of a "happy accident".

How to Use this Book

This book can be read through cover to cover or you may decide that you would like to focus on one specific area of Team Mastery and so pick out that chapter to read and reflect on.

After the stories, there is a section of perforated pages containing the milestone cards – each card is colour coded and contains symbols in the upper-left corner that correspond to the associated characteristics. These cards can be torn out of the book to use for photo opportunities, to stick in a team journal or to decorate the team space as and when you reach them.

Many teams will choose one milestone to work towards and then, when good progress is made in that area, pick another one to focus on. Others will look through the milestone cards every few weeks and see which ones they have met or are close to meeting.

I also include a number of blank milestone cards where you can capture your own important moments of team growth. Get creative, add your own hashtag and share to the rest of the community on social media with the #TeamMastery hashtag.

Geoff Watts
Author

S

SQUAD

Self-Improvement

"There is only one corner of the universe you can be certain of improving, and that's your own self."

Aldous Huxley

Self-Improvement

One of the principles behind the Manifesto for Agile Software Development [1] states that:

"At regular intervals, the team reflects on how to become more effective, then tunes and adjusts its behavior accordingly."

This principle of inspection and adaptation is at the heart of empiricism which, in turn, is at the heart of agility. Although teams are constantly striving to get work "done", the individuals on that team are never done improving and the team itself is never done in their pursuit of mastery.

Self-improvement, at the team level, is most often realised in the practice of retrospectives, a period of time set aside on a regular basis for a team to inspect and adapt their working practices. Time set aside specifically for self-improvement is rightly seen as a hallmark of agile delivery.

Because, historically, many teams in organisations have not had a regular opportunity for improvement, many consider this a "benefit" of agile delivery. Because of the fundamental philosophy of inspection and adaptation in the agile manifesto, it is equally valid to consider a practice such as the retrospective to be a "responsibility" of an agile team.

Of course, just having a retrospective is no guarantee of positive change; a team has to put something into practice [Card SC1]. Before action is taken though, one of the first steps to self-improvement is for teams to become aware that it is possible, and to feel safe in identifying and making improvements.

Many teams, or individuals on teams, are uncomfortable with the concept of continuous improvement at first. Acknowledging that a gap exists between where we currently are and where we could be can be unsettling because it implies that we are not already good. Pointing out that the team have a skills gap can damage individual egos and create resistance to change from within. People sometimes react defensively, perhaps blaming the system or lack of opportunity in order to justify our current state.

Worse still, some people mistakenly believe that skills are an inherent, unchangeable facet of each individual's character that cannot be changed. Carol Dweck describes this as a "fixed mindset" [2], a major inhibitor to development and change.

Great teams realise that there is an alternative to a fixed mindset; the "growth mindset" [Card SC2]. A growth mindset, according to Dweck, is a belief that our intelligence and ability is not fixed; that we can become more intelligent and tackle new problems with the right mindset. Dweck's research showed that once school-aged students were exposed to the fact that intelligence is malleable and that the brain can grow with effort, their math grades increased significantly. Just knowing you can change is half the battle.

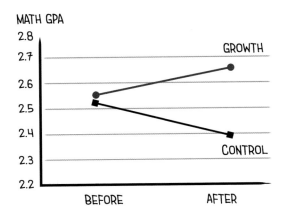

MATH GRADES BEFORE & AFTER INTERVENTION

In the workplace, great teams apply this principle of growth mindset when faced with complex problems. Because great teams believe they have the ability to find a solution, they are better able to do so.

Great teams also know that showing appreciation for hard work and effort rather than pure intelligence or skill promotes a growth mindset. People are more willing to take on difficult challenges in the first place when they know that their efforts will be appreciated.

A by-product of a growth mindset is resilience. By believing that we have the capacity to learn from our experiences, we don't give up when faced with setbacks but rather continue to work at a solution. Angela Duckworth, one of Dweck's students, coined the term "grit" [3] after researching the importance of perseverance in student performance [Card SC3].

People with a fixed mindset, when faced with a setback, will often adopt a stance of "I can't do this" compared to a healthier growth mindset response of "I haven't found out how to do it yet".

Great teams know that practising self-improvement frees them to reach not only their combined potential but also their individual potential. Once teams get into the habit of self-improvement, and begin to prove to themselves that it is possible, they can see outside of their immediate sphere of influence and perceive the wider system.

In the following story, we meet the Apocasprint team who are in a retrospective. Sasha, the ScrumMaster, Abe the Product Owner, and team members Rosita, Eugene, Rick, Michonne and Lori are trying to figure out how to improve their cycle time and find that a growth mindset is helpful to them in doing that.

Grow Your Team, Grow Your Influence

A good team improves themselves.
A great team improves the system.

"One thing that keeps coming up in our retrospectives is that our cycle time is too long. It's taking us months to return requests to the customer. To be competitive, we need to find ways to make that weeks," said Sasha, ScrumMaster of the Apocasprint team. "I'd like to suggest we spend this time looking for some ways to address our cycle time."

"I agree," said one of the team members, Rosita. "It's taking far too long for us to respond to requests from our customers. That's got to change if we want to grow our business and be able to land exciting new contracts."

Their Product Owner, Abe, who Sasha had invited to the retrospective, agreed. "I can only use the 'we're a new company' excuse for so long. I know you are all working as hard as you can, but we need to find ways to deliver products to our customers more reliably."

The team brainstormed solutions and decided to start by improving their workflow with the goal of reducing cycle time. They created a new work board to capture and track their process. Once complete, the board had sixteen columns. It looked daunting, but the team believed it **should** look daunting because the work itself was complex and somewhat overwhelming.

"We all know how to use this, correct?" asked Sasha. "Whenever a card is in the Analysis Out column, that means one of the developers can pull it and start building stuff. Then, when it is in the Dev Out column, any of the testers can pull it and start testing it and so on."

"And Abe has broken the work items down to such small blocks that anyone should only really be working on any of them for a day or two max," added Eugene, one of the developers.

That first two weeks went really well; everyone was busy and they liked seeing the cards move across the board. Towards the end of the sprint, though, there was clearly a bottleneck beginning to appear in the Dev Out column.

At the retrospective meeting, where the team reflected on how things were going and how they could be improved, Rosita was the first to speak.

"Guys, I know that was a good sprint for most of you, but I was completely overwhelmed," Rosita said. "If we are going to carry on like this, we are going to need more testing help to cope with the workload."

"There was definitely more pressure on you than anyone else, but would extra testers really be the answer?" questioned Lori, an analyst on the team.

"I think Lori's right," said Eugene. "All we would be doing is shifting the bottleneck. It's a Theory of Constraints thing." [4]

"Can you tell us more about that?" asked Sasha.

Eugene went up to the task board and gestured as he explained. "The Theory of Constraints is a management paradigm that advocates throttling the throughput of work—slowing everything down to the speed of the bottleneck in the process. So during our sprint, a bottleneck formed here, at Dev Out, but none of us stopped what we were doing in other areas of the process to help relieve the bottleneck or slowed down our work to reduce the bottleneck. And according to the Theory of Constraints, we should have. There is no point in producing work that the bottleneck does not have the capacity to process."

"I've heard of that," said Lori. "We're supposed to slow down to speed up. But what do we do while we aren't working?"

Eugene answered, "Although it might seem counterintuitive, idle time is sometimes a good thing. The process should revolve around the constraining part until things can be changed to make that constraint no longer constraining. And one thing we can do to help is to reduce the batch size."

"You've lost me," said Rosita.

Most of the other team members nodded in agreement.

Map the Workflow

"I know a cool game that might help us with this," Eugene continued, and then produced a handful of coins from his pocket.

Eugene walked the team through The Penny Game [5] so that they could experience how different batch sizes in the workflow affect the throughput of work within a development process. Every team member acted out a part in a pretend system with the goal of flipping coins before passing the coins to the next person who would also then flip them. Each individual was timed how long it took them to flip their coins while the total time taken for everyone to flip the coins was also measured.

The exercise showed that as batch sizes (the number of coins someone would flip before passing them on down the line) reduced, the time taken by each individual to flip their coins increased while the total time to flip all the coins decreased. This is because the team had shifted from each individual focusing on their own production towards focusing on getting value through the system.

"I think we may be too focused on doing our own little bit of the process and not focused enough on getting a piece of work through the whole system," suggested Eugene. "If we track how we handle a piece of work from start to finish, we could see where it spends more time and where it gets held up. Then, we could see if reducing our batch sizes or work in process limits helps the overall throughput time."

The team then followed a typical piece of work through their board of sixteen columns to identify where the value-add time and waste time was within their current set-up, with Eugene introducing the rest of the team to techniques such as Value Stream Mapping [6] and Causal Loop Diagrams [7].

One area of inefficiency jumped out at them straight away.

For each piece of work, Lori would do her bit of analysis and then move it to the Analysis Out column. Every day, at their daily huddle, one of the developers, such as Eugene, would pick it up. But sometimes half a day passed between the time Lori moved the card to the Analysis Out column and when a developer picked it up. And in the meantime, Lori might have completed a second card and added it to the column.

The delay in pick-up meant, in essence, that the developers' batch size was often two cards instead of one.

The team found similar delays in handoffs at each column of the board. They quickly realised that the work in process got larger the further to the right of the board they got and, because she was the last step in the process, Rosita was the most over-burdened.

"But I don't see how we can change things in our set-up," Michonne said before correcting herself. "Sorry … I mean to say, I'm sure we can optimise our workflow somehow; we just haven't figured it out yet."

"Nice catch, Michonne," said Lori. "There's that growth mindset in action!"

> ### *In what specific area would it be beneficial for you to adopt a growth mindset?*

"Well, one way that teams have reduced their batch size is by something called The Three Amigos [8] where for each card, an analyst, a developer and a tester work together to complete the work," said Eugene. "Perhaps we could give that a try?"

This experiment had the effect of condensing six columns on their board down to two, because so many handoffs (and time delays) were eliminated. As a result, "cycle time" was reduced from ten days to just over seven.

This was the spark for the team. Over the next six months, they identified opportunities to condense their board into fewer columns, reducing their cycle time more and more. They were so motivated to improve their process that they were even removing their own impediments rather than simply raising them for someone else to tackle them. [Card SC4]

To Win or to Lose?

About that time, their Product Owner, Abe, came to them with a request to pitch for a huge contract from a potential new client. The Apocasprint team, along with the accounts team, the sales team, and the CIO and COO, worked for weeks on the tender. But on the day before the pitch was due, the team met with everyone involved and said that they had made the decision not to pitch.

Sasha explained, "After working the numbers, we've realised that we cannot deploy frequently enough to meet the client's deadlines."

The room fell silent.

"We feel gutted," Sasha continued. "It is such an exciting project and was for just the kind of client we've been seeking."

"I'm just so disappointed," said Eugene. "This contract would have boosted us to a new level. I hate having to say no."

"We've looked at it from every angle, though," added Michonne. "We couldn't have made the timeline and would have had to go back to them to renegotiate later. Disappointing a client like that would ruin our chances for future contracts in that market. It was the right thing to do."

"It just feels like all the work we've done to improve has been for nothing," Eugene replied.

Abe couldn't completely hide his frustration.

"I thought you had been reducing cycle times over the last few months. I don't understand why we are still unable to meet these deadlines." he said.

"That's what I mean when I say it feels like what we've done has been for nothing," said Eugene. "We've cut our lead time by more than half—but it wasn't enough."

Sasha addressed the group, "We have come a long way and removed a lot of bottlenecks. But what we've realised through these contract discussions is that we have a new bottleneck – deployment."

"You're right," explained Lori. "We've been measuring cycle time, but we weren't actually measuring the *full* cycle time because we weren't including the deployment process in that measure!"

Rick, the COO, jumped in. "OK, I'm responsible for this company meeting growth targets – targets that we are not going to hit as things stand. And what you have told me is that the deployment process is the main thing that stands between us and winning contracts like the one we just had to let go."

The team nodded.

"Right. Well I'm going to go on record now as saying our number one priority is to be able to make changes to our products and systems faster and safer," Rick added. "We need to get back to the days when our account managers could get customer requests back to customers in a matter of weeks not months."

"Hear hear!" shouted Abe.

"If anyone has any ideas for how to do this, I want to hear them. I'll give you two weeks to come up with a plan," added Rick, before he got up and left.

The rest of the team looked at each other and there was silence for a few seconds before Sasha said:

"I love the fact that you all, like me, are so clearly gutted about not being able to tender for this piece of work and I want you to really internalise that bad feeling. Not because I think we should feel shame or guilt but because I want us to make a commitment that this will be the last time we feel like that. Speaking for myself, I'm determined to get into a position where we don't have to turn away great work again."

"I agree," said Eugene. "And I think I know where to start."

"I've got some ideas too," said Lori.

"Right. So let's all come in tomorrow and put our heads together to figure out what we need to do to tackle the deployment issue. We did it with testing so we can do it for deployment too," challenged Sasha.

Great Teams Think Bigger Than Themselves

The next day, team Apocasprint ran a workshop, including members of the deployment team, where they identified four metrics to improve:

- deployment frequency
- change failure rate
- mean time to recovery
- lead time for changes.

"If we're going to make progress in these areas, we'll first need to get some data about the current state of things. It might not be pretty but we need to have a benchmark," suggested Rosita.

> *What data would you like to*
> *capture and make a plan to improve?*

Over the next week, volunteers from all over the department, and some outside, started gathering data. They measured overall cycle time from past work items, they measured how often deployments got rejected, and how quickly changes were implemented. Through this process, they discovered some surprising and, frankly, worrying things. For example, many teams weren't following the standard automated deployment processes.

The Apocasprint team had gone from focusing on optimising their own process to looking at the wider "system" [Card SC5]. They realised that optimising locally only had a limited scope for overall improvement, and sometimes could be detrimental to the overall system. By looking at the end-to-end process – which was outside of their official remit – they were able to identify significant opportunities for the organisation to increase their capacity to deliver.

But it wasn't easy.

At the end of Rick's two-week investigation timebox, there was a "Town Hall" meeting where anyone who had proposals for "making change faster and safer" could pitch their ideas. If they were good, and needed backing, he and the senior leadership team would decide whether to support them or not.

Sasha presented the benchmark metrics with slight embarrassment before suggesting that the development teams adopt a number of engineering practices (including test automation, continuous integration and cloud-based services), to increase their deployment frequency from four to thirty times a month. It would involve a lot of learning on the part of the team but they all had an appetite for it [Card SC6].

She also presented a prototype of a heat map of technical debt to visualise where issues were in the overall development process and a commitment to gradually turning the red dots green.

Rick was impressed and asked how much it would cost him.

"To be honest, we don't know," said Sasha, "but our plan is to measure our progress every two weeks and see how much return on investment we get for each mini-investment. For example, we would like to start with a team training session on the engineering practices and some extra slack in the next couple of sprints to embed them. At the end of the next sprint, we'll compare the changes in the heat map to see if it's been worth it."

Rick agreed.

This was the beginning of what was to become a perpetual state of intrinsically motivated self-betterment. The team appeared to become addicted to beating their own personal bests on the metrics they had identified.

> *Which metrics would you like to
> beat your personal bests in?*

It's no surprise that the team in this story became more and more motivated to improve. Indeed, all three elements of Daniel Pink's Motivation 3.0 [9] are in play in this story. The first element is a clear, motivating purpose and the team wanted to put themselves in a position where they would never have to turn away great work again. The second aspect of Motivation 3.0 is autonomy and the team were given the chance to figure out how to achieve the goal. The third aspect of mastery was also present, as the team were able to see themselves become better at what they were doing.

All of the great teams I have seen have a similar story to tell. They don't improve because managers tell them to, or because they are offered a bonus to improve. They want to improve because that is an innate driver of human motivation. When people don't appear to have this driver, it is often because something key is missing. Either they are missing a clear purpose (or a purpose that matches their personal values), they are lacking autonomy (or the support to make their autonomy count) or they aren't supported in their development towards mastery.

When teams have purpose, autonomy and mastery in place but still aren't striving for self-improvement, the number one factor undermining this, in my experience, is fear. This fear could be about judgement, or failure, or of upsetting people, or many other types of fear. If people are fearful, they struggle to act and so creating an environment of psychological safety [10] is critical for a team to develop.

If fear is stopping you or your team-mates from tapping into your intrinsic motivators then look at the stories in the Audacity section for help.

SUMMARY

Great teams:

- Slow down to speed up
- Believe they can learn any skill given time
- Don't give up easily
- Have a strong sense of psychological safety
- Think bigger than themselves

TRY THIS:

Think of a skill or capability that you would like to have as a team. Assume you can achieve it and set about developing it. Make a commitment to keep trying for six months.

Earlier, I described one way to look at the retrospective is that the constant inspecting and adapting of a team's working practices is a responsibility, i.e. you cannot be considered agile unless you are determining how to get better as a team every couple of weeks [Card SC1].

This is a conscious thing for many good teams, but one sign of a great team is when they are improving almost consistently and it becomes just one part of how they work.

Of course, when something becomes mandatory or a responsibility then it begins to feel like a chore and is less fun or impactful, but I would argue that self-improvement is a necessary discipline for a team to be great. It is certainly a characteristic of every great team I have seen or been part of.

Great teams also find ways to make improvement NOT feel like a chore and, perhaps unconsciously, take inspiration from Mary Poppins' famous quote:

"In every job that must be done, there is an element of fun. You find the fun and – SNAP – the job's a game."

Self-improvement is a discipline, but it is also an intrinsic motivation for the great teams I have witnessed; they enjoy getting better and better. They enjoy beating their own previous personal best [Card SC7] and view standing still as stagnating or even falling behind.

Teams on their journey to mastery often progress from the formal improvements made at retrospectives to more informal, ad-hoc improvements [Card SC8] made the moment they become apparent. I have observed teams making improvements to their working practices so organically that their retrospectives became the time when they took stock of all the improvements they had made during the sprint (so as not to lose track of their efforts) rather than making a plan for what they would do.

In the beginning, improvements to the team's working practices can be quite dramatic and often have game-changing effects on performance. Eventually, though, great teams realise that to be truly effective, improvements also need to be made at the system level.

In a similar way, the changes teams make to themselves and the system as they are beginning their journey to mastery tend to be larger and immediately impactful. But once those improvements have been made, great teams start to focus on marginal gains; the seemingly small changes that begin to perfect their performance.

The following is a story of such a team. Danesh and the rest of team Peloton are attempting to help Product Owner Lily and Sales and Account Managers Collette, Kiara, and Martí who are experiencing issues with how the product Peloton built actually works in practice for them. Once team Peloton had solved that challenge, Tom and the team found that sometimes it's the small things that make a big difference.

Change Big, Change Small

A good team makes the big, game-changing improvements.
A great team makes many small,
game-perfecting improvements.

"Yes, sure… hold on and I'll get it for you," Danesh said to the person at the other end of the phone. "Got it. I will email that over to you now. Say, Collette, out of morbid curiosity, how long did it take to create the report when you tried it yourself?" he asked. "Wow – and after all that time you couldn't generate it? I'm really sorry about that."

Danesh had been manually retrieving the daily shipment reconciliation report for Collette almost every day now. The user experience (UX) had deteriorated so badly that it now took over eight minutes for a user to create the essential report that just four months ago had taken thirty seconds. Worse, the report often failed to generate and had to be manually retrieved by the development team.

Danesh raised the issue with the team at their daily meeting and he wasn't the only one performing work-arounds for the users and customer account managers. It was getting to the point where the team couldn't add any more features because they were so busy dealing with issues.

The Peloton team was relatively new, having been formed from members of different functional departments three months ago in the hope that a cross-functional team would reduce the amount of time taken to get features completed. By having all the skills in the same team, the number of handoffs between the functional areas had been reduced, so it took significantly less time to deliver something end to end than before.

But none of those changes had solved the UX issues.

The team had been trying for weeks to reduce the number of UX problem tickets, but no matter how many problems they solved, the list kept getting longer instead of shorter. The product was old and had been patched together over many years without consideration for how the upgrades fitted together; and it was the UX that was suffering the most.

Team morale was getting low.

Danesh looked around at his team, "We've got the monthly review coming up this afternoon. I'm not sure I can handle two hours of listening to our users complain about UX problems and us not having any answers. Can we have a huddle to come up with some solutions? It's not just affecting our productivity; it's affecting my motivation at work most days. And I'm fairly certain it's affecting you too."

The team agreed. During the huddle, one thing they discussed was how things seemed to have been getting worse for some time. It was almost as though, despite their best efforts, their productivity (and fulfilment) was dropping every day. They decided they would make one more pitch to the stakeholders to let them re-engineer the front-end framework.

At the review meeting, Danesh explained their progress (or lack of) during the last two weeks, describing the fixes they had put in place before explaining how frustrated they felt for the users because the product was just so unwieldy.

"We can really empathise with the users and we are doing everything we can to help them but it's just not enough. I know it isn't something you want to hear, but this product really needs some investment. We have been talking as a team and we are happy to try and keep the lights on while replacing the front-end framework. What do you think?"

> *How well can you empathise with the*
> *challenge of your users?*

"Well I would definitely support it," Kiara, a sales manager, said. "I've lost three major clients this month to our competitor because they are fed up with the unreliability of the report generation."

"I have to admit it's making it much harder to win pitches at the moment," Martí added "and, let's be honest, it's not like we are getting many of our new feature requests built at the moment anyway!"

"We believe there are at least five different frameworks out there that could improve things significantly. We don't know which one is the best one but, to be honest, any of them is better than what we have right now," Danesh said.

Experiment in Complexity

"I would like to suggest that we try all five frameworks in some short experiments based on our customers' biggest problems and see which works the best, then go with that one. Investigating multiple options may seem like an expensive approach but when the right answer is not self-evident, it gives us the best chance of finding out what it is." [Card AC10]

"In principle, I think we probably need to bite the bullet here," agreed Lily, the product manager. "But, we can't risk it on the shipment reconciliation report. If we make changes to that and it gets worse, then we are in real trouble. We have no guarantee that making the change to any of these new frameworks will be better."

"I understand the shipment reconciliation report is too risky and that's fine because we can test the frameworks on some of the smaller reports first. If it were me deciding then I would be trying to convince some of our real users to get involved in the testing and benchmark where things are right now, in terms of things they care about such as responsiveness, completeness and personalisation. I would probably offer them a year's free licencing for their trouble," Danesh offered.

Lily was convinced to give it a try and, over the next few weeks, half the team continued fighting fires while the other half worked with users to get feedback on the frameworks. They narrowed them down from five to three and then two when Lily felt confident enough to test them both on the shipment reconciliation report.

At this point, the CTO got wind of the experiments and became involved, stating that because of re-training and recruitment costs one of the frameworks was a much better choice than the other. The experiments had proven the worth of changing the front-end framework and, over the next few months, the UX improved dramatically.

This re-engineering was not only valuable to the product in the short term but it also gave the Peloton team a taste for continual improvement, a common trait amongst great teams.

Fast forward six months. Team Peloton had improved greatly in more areas than just the product's UX and were now considered one of the best teams in the organisation. One morning, the team were discussing the cycling at the Olympics and Tom – a keen cyclist within the team – brought up the topic of marginal gains.

The "Aggregation of Marginal Gains"

The "aggregation of marginal gains" is a term that was first associated with British Cycling and, in particular, a coach Dave Brailsford [11]. Brailsford was brought in to transform the under-performing team of British cyclists and his method was not to change any one thing drastically but rather to change everything a little bit.

He theorised that if everything that goes into winning a race is improved by just one percent then the overall impact would end up being immense. From obvious changes like improving the design of the seats for greater comfort to abstract changes such as improving the way cyclists washed their hands to reduce the chances of getting sick. Everything!

Those little changes had a profound impact. Just five years after Brailsford took over, the British Cycling team dominated the road and track cycling events at the 2008 Olympic Games in Beijing, where they won an astounding 60 percent of the gold medals available. Four years later, when the Olympic Games came to London, Team GB raised the bar as they set nine Olympic records and seven world records.

When you look at the underlying maths, it isn't surprising. If your performance is 100 units on day zero and you improved one percent every day for a whole year, then your performance at the end of the year would be 3,778 units.

$$1.01^{365} = 37.78$$

1 % BETTER
EVERY DAY

Ref: jamesclear.com

THE POWER OF TINY GAINS

Tom wondered if the team could implement this principle and commit to making one tiny improvement every day rather than one big improvement at a retrospective [Card SC9].

In their next retrospective, instead of looking for an obvious area of opportunity to improve, team Peloton decided to look for things that they already did well but might be able to improve even more. To begin with, the team tweaked the time and length of their meetings to see what the optimum was for them, they tried different venues for their meetings and had lunch together once a week; they even experimented with different brands of coffee in the office.

> ### *What do you already do well as a team*
> ### *but could improve slightly?*

They created a board for ideas as and when they came to people, but sometimes people would just announce in the morning meeting what they would like to try that day. They kept a lightweight journal to keep track of what they did, what worked and what didn't, and would review it at the end of each week to solidify their growth.

After seeing some positive results from their changes, their improvements stepped up a level as they began running parallel experiments on their development tasks and got a neutral expert to review their use of tools.

To begin with, they slipped up often – they forgot things or broke their habits, but they regrouped and went again. [See the story on *Embracing Candour,* p124, for more on this.]

It took discipline, grit and a lot of conscious effort to start and maintain the habit of continuous improvement. It was impossible for them to tell if they had increased by 3,778 percent as the theory of one percent marginal gains would suggest, but they had seen impressive improvements nonetheless.

Team Peloton dramatically cut the amount of time it took to create value and get it in the hands of their customers. They were delivering more work as a team despite focusing less on ensuring each member of the team was busy all of the time. There were less tangible benefits as well in terms of creativity and general happiness.

One effective way of embedding a new habit that team Peloton employed was attaching the new habit to an existing habit. Find something that you have managed to ritualise without thinking (for example, brushing your teeth) and then attach another habit to that. For example, the team regularly asked themselves three questions every morning in their Daily Scrum, so it was easy enough to get into a new habit by adding a fourth question of "What experiment are we running today?"

Tom also came in one day with a poster of a group of people rowing and stuck it on the team wall. On the poster were the words "Will It Make The Boat Go Faster?" [12] and he told the story of the Team GB rowing team who went from failing to make the final of major regattas to Olympic Champions by ruthlessly following this motto.

When deciding whether or not to do something, the rowers would ask themselves the question "Will it Make The Boat Go Faster?" If the answer was "no" then they simply would not do it. Even to the point of deciding not to attend the once in a lifetime Olympic Opening Ceremony.

Tom suggested the team adopt something similar and also consider using some specific language to help make their new habits stick. For their retrospective actions, the team experimented with the structure suggested by B.J. Fogg, author of "tiny habits" [13], who suggests that commitments be written in the following format:

"After I ..., I will ..."

One example of this was when team Peloton made a team commitment to adopting some quiet time to make their mornings more productive.

"After we have our daily meeting, we will have
a thirty-minute 'Peaceful Progress' session."

Fogg suggests you should make the commitment as small as you possibly can. So, for example, instead of saying, "After I brush my teeth, I will floss my teeth," you would say, "After I brush my teeth, I will floss **one** tooth." After performing this tiny commitment for five days, you almost always increase the amount of flossing you do without changing your commitment.

**What small improvement could
you introduce and attach to an existing ritual?**

The psychology behind this method is that by reducing the commitment to something tiny, the brain doesn't subconsciously resist. And then, when you add on a reward for doing it, you reinforce that positive behaviour with a positive emotion. I discuss this in more detail in the introduction to the next section, *Quality [see p52]*.

Team Peloton used this technique to make changes to their habits much easier to ritualise.

For more information on motivation for change, see the section on my Change Equation in the introduction to *Audacity [see p120]*.

Team Improvement Models

When it comes to facilitating a team's improvement there are a couple of models that I have seen used to help.

The first is the CDE model [14] which was created by Human System Dynamics expert Glenda Eoyang. She proposed three conditions that affect how patterns of human dynamics emerge. The great teams that I have seen have experimented with these conditions to enhance their teamwork.

C stands for Containers that the team are operating within. The organisation is a container, the team itself is a container, the project is a kind of container; anything that distinguishes the system from its surroundings and helps hold it together is a container and playing with the containers and their definitions can have interesting results.

D stands for Differences. All great teams have a great diversity and these differences can generate a positive tension that can stimulate and accelerate growth. Increasing or decreasing the amount of difference is another lever that great teams can play with to their advantage.

Differences is an interesting dynamic in self-organising teams. Solomon Asch ran a fascinating experiment into groupthink [15] and found that people are unlikely to state the truth if all of their colleagues unanimously agree on the wrong option. However, having just one different opinion, even if that is another incorrect opinion, opens people up to airing their true views. Great teams will do whatever it takes to encourage critical evaluation, even if it means one person deliberately offering an incorrect assessment at times.

Finally, E stands for Exchanges and refers to the various parts of the system (in the context of a team, the team members) interacting with one another. Different exchanges can lead to different dynamics and so playing with who interacts with whom and in what context can also lead to enhanced teamwork.

Some teams will look to a facilitator or catalyst to help them play with these levers of team dynamics but great teams get to a point where they can do this facilitation themselves [Card SC10].

The second model that I have seen great teams work with is ABIDE [16]. ABIDE is similar to CDE but has a few more aspects to it. It stands for:

Attractors   – what makes it attractive to be part of this team?
Barriers   – what are the limits of acceptable behaviour that,
               if breached, mean expulsion from the team?
Identities   – people may fill multiple roles within the team
               – what are they and who will fill them?

Diversity   – how can we encourage constructive dissent
                and difference?

Environment – how could we alter the physical, psychological
                or cultural environment for our benefit?

Regardless of the model, great teams look at everything they can do
to enhance their ability to continue improving either through large,
revolutionary enhancements to change the game or those seemingly
tiny, yet perfecting enhancements. Of course, perfect never lasts and
so there is no end state for the great teams. There will always be a need
for a team to reassess and go again. This is an inspiring and motivating
thought for the great teams I have known.

SUMMARY

Great teams:

- Empathise with users and customers
- Experiment to solve problems and build confidence
- Establish a habit of continual improvement
- Understand that little tweaks can be really powerful
- Focus on making "the boat" go faster

TRY THIS:

Create a metaphor for your team similar to "the boat" and challenge yourself to identify one small way to "make it faster" every day.

SQUAD

Quality

"Quality is not an act, it is a habit."

Aristotle

Quality

Building high-quality products and services requires discipline and, at times, we may ask ourselves if it would really hurt if we just let things slip a little. Great teams though, without question, take pride in doing things well. I have often said that it is very easy to build a bad product because it's just so tempting and easy to cut a corner here and there. This is why my favourite principle of the agile manifesto is the one that states:

> *"Continuous attention to technical excellence and good design enhances agility."*

This principle strongly resonates with great teams as well. When you think about anything that has been done to a level of excellence, you will undoubtedly find that discipline and attention to detail tend to be major components behind that, and great teams do their chores … regularly.

Building in quality involves a good deal of humility because it means being open to the possibility of not doing something well. Great teams are conscientious but not perfectionists. Wanting to do something the best we can is a good thing but it must not paralyse us into thinking it must be perfect.

Great teams realise they don't have the luxury of building something perfect; they simply won't have the time or, likely, the budget for that. Just as there is no excuse for shoddy workmanship, there is no excuse for over-gilding the proverbial lily.

Great teams display a high level of conscience because a lot of the "quality" can be hidden, so our customers may not easily notice that there is a quality deficiency – certainly in the short term. But they will notice eventually. Just as when a sports team slacks off on their practice or their fitness training, when a software team slacks off on their testing, the consequences may not become evident for a few weeks or even months; but they will, and great teams have a very strong moral compass when it comes to the integrity of not just what they do but how they do it.

Do great sports teams miss a training session now and again? Sure. Do great software teams push something to the live environment knowing there is a bug in the code? Maybe, once or twice. But these great teams are aware of the consequences of doing so on technical integrity and user goodwill so don't let it become a habit. They tend to feel guilty about it and double down their efforts to recover the situation. The habit that great teams get into is one of *improving* the state of their product rather than making it worse.

Our first "quality" story looks at the Avengers team who managed to raise their own bar of quality. Francesca, Nasser, Hudson and Jalilah take quality very seriously and are keen to help Elliot, the Product Owner, maintain the integrity of his product. But, when they meet call centre agent Raluca, they decide that fixing what goes wrong sometimes isn't enough.

See Bug, Fix Bug, Inoculate

A good team reacts to fix what goes wrong.
A great team proactively raises the bar.

"Hello. Francesca speaking ... Oh, hi Elliot ... yes ... ok ... I see ... and what exactly does it say?"

Elliot was the Product Owner for team Avengers. Francesca, one of the developers, looks to Nasser, one of her team-mates and calmly nods before writing the word "family" on a sticky note for him to see before continuing talking with her caller. "Sure, we will put it on the board and get back to you shortly. Thanks for letting me know and tell them we are sorry for the inconvenience."

"Avengers assemble!" Francesca almost shouts, and the rest of the team jump up and gather together in a sort-of huddle.

"That was Elliot," she explains. "He's found an issue in the new feature we rolled out on Tuesday. A number of the call centre agents are getting some error messages that mean some of the data they are capturing are getting lost."

The Avengers team had a policy known as the M:I Matrix for deciding which defects they would work on immediately and which ones would have to wait.

% USERS AFFECTED

M:I MATRIX	MINORITY	MIDDLING	MAJORITY
ITCHY	STRANGER	COLLEAGUES	FRIENDS
INCONVENIENT	COLLEAGUES	FRIENDS	FAMILY
INTOLERABLE	FRIENDS	FAMILY	CELEBRITIES

(SEVERITY labels the vertical axis)

The word "Family" is the team's agreed way of referring to an issue that needs to be fixed now. The team doesn't argue about whether something is a bug or a change request or a new requirement. It's just another piece of important work – the key is to determine how important. If the word Francesca had used was "Friends" or "Colleagues", they would have treated that issue differently. They would have either put it off until the next sprint or put it in the "flagged pile", tagged so they would notice it whenever they worked on that area of the product next.

The issue was mapped to the table above, depending on the number of people it was affecting and the severity of the problem. This was then agreed with Elliot, the Product Owner.

Mike Cohn refers to this as "Prioritisation By Policy" [1] and great teams almost always have something like this in place.

"If you let me know the users then I can pull up the logs," says Hudson, keen as always to get going straight away.

"Hold on a minute. What have we got in progress? When's best to look at this?" Francesca asks.

"First thing after lunch I think," says Jalilah, another member of the team, "but I think we should let Elliot know that one of the new features is going to be pushed back."

"He already expects that to be the case," says Francesca, "but he's OK with it because he was expecting a few teething issues."

This calm approach is a far cry from the panic a few months ago when everything seemed to be on fire. Back then they had very little strategy to their work and, because of this, everything was a high priority. This scattergun approach led to nothing being done properly and so the team ended up revisiting the same problem time and again.

Because of this, the team took the brave step of deciding to fix everything they became aware of as a team. They didn't want to create individual pockets of product knowledge or abandon one person to the soul-less role of support, so they did what many great teams do and employed a "stop and swarm" mentality. [Card QC1]

Good teams know who to direct traffic to when there is a specific issue, but great teams take a collective approach and quality is so important to them that they will almost always stop what they are doing and ruthlessly eliminate that bug – as a team.

It was during one of these swarming sessions that Nasser jokingly commented, "Wouldn't it be great if we could hit bug zero?" [Card QC2]

"What's bug zero?" Jalilah asked.

"I was joking, but I recently hit inbox zero where I had no unread emails and it felt so good that I wondered if it was possible to get to bug zero," Nasser explained.

"I would LOVE that!" exclaimed Jalilah.

"Me too," added Francesca, "and I bet Elliot would too. But that just doesn't seem possible."

"Maybe it isn't possible, but we could still aim for it though, right?" suggested Nasser.

"Yeah. Maybe we start by employing the Boy Scout Rule and see where it takes us," added Hudson, another of the developers who started to get excited by this idea that was forming within the team.

"What's the Boy Scout Rule?" asked Jalilah.

> *"Leave this world a little better than you found it."*
> ~ Robert Baden Powell

"Well," replied Hudson, "the Boy Scout Movement had a principle to leave the campsite (and the world) in a better state than they found it. Robert C. Martin, signatory of the Manifesto for Agile Software Development [2], suggested that software developers should follow Baden Powell's advice and coined the term the Boy Scout Rule imploring developers to leave the code cleaner than they found it."

As well as swarming to fix what they were made aware of, team Avengers then made a commitment to each other to always leave the product in a better state [CARD QC3] than when they found it. Every time they worked on an aspect of the product, they would look for anything that could be streamlined, fixed or enhanced – and I mean every time. It was one of their rituals.

This inevitably led to every member of the team being needed to work on something that was not their speciality. I have heard the phrase "Testers test and developers develop; that's how it's always been" many times, but as a great team, the Avengers did not buy into this.

It takes a great team spirit and a psychologically safe environment that encourages and supports breadth of knowledge, but I have rarely seen a great team where there hasn't been a conscious effort to build in resilience by cross-skilling.

To begin with, it was hard for the team to convince Elliot to back them up on this stance. He was paying for the product after all and this seemed like a slow-down in their approach. Eventually Francesca showed Elliot the data demonstrating how much time the team were spending revisiting work items and suggested an experiment:

If we spend ten percent more time on this piece of work than we would normally have estimated, we predict that we will not need to come back to it for at least three months.

During the experiment, when the team looked back at the number of trouble tickets raised, the hours of debugging, and other specific, measurable costs, the business case for doing things to a higher standard was quite stark and Elliot didn't take much convincing, but the experimental approach certainly helped to make it easier for him.

> **What could you try to make it easier for doubters to see the benefit of higher quality?**

What is a Bug?

"What do you mean, you can't add that to the main customer policy? We fixed that bug a couple of months ago," Nasser said. "You just go to the add-ons screen and select it."

"Oh, that's easy for you to say Nas, but when we are in the flow of a customer call we can't access that screen without losing the data we have input from the start of the call," Raluca responded. "We get so many of them now after this campaign was launched last month. We can't cope and it's ending up in so many customer complaints because we mess up the manual workaround we have."

"I had no idea. We were just told we needed to give you an option to add the extra cover to the main policy and we did. Elliot signed it off so we assumed that bug was fixed," Nasser said, feeling sorry for his friend.

"Well it might be fixed for you, but it's not fixed for us. Come up tomorrow and I'll show you. You can listen in to a customer call if you like," Raluca offered.

"I will. And I'll bring the team. It's been a long time since we've got to see the system in actual use," Nasser replied.

The next day, in the team's morning meeting, Nasser suggested they all follow him on a mini field-trip up to the seventh floor. When he got there he nodded at Raluca who was already on a customer call and she waved them over to her station.

"Absolutely sir, it's great that you would like to take advantage of this month's offer and add this cover to your policy. I just need to take a few details," Raluca said professionally before scribbling the customer details onto sticky notes on her desk.

"Why is she using sticky notes?" asked Jalilah.

"Shall I show her the add-ons screen?" asked Hudson, stepping forward and reaching for Raluca's mouse.

"Hold on Hudson," said Nasser, "She knows the screen is there but she can't access it without losing all of the data she has entered so far."

"But look at all of those sticky notes!" Jalilah said, aghast that Raluca had to go through this workaround process.

"I guess she hasn't had time to update the system between calls," Nasser pondered. "And we thought this was fixed. Have you checked social media recently? The number of complaints is high but I don't think Elliot knows that we could fix this really easily and it would have such a big impact."

On the way back down to their work area, the team stopped by Elliot's office and spoke to him about what they had noticed. They suggested that the "Add-on fix" be re-opened and asked to work on it straight away.

Once Elliot agreed, Nasser asked if they could include Raluca in their fix because she knows the user experience and this would allow them to fix the bug from the customer perspective as well as from a technical perspective.

It took some persuading but Elliot called in a favour and managed to negotiate half a day of Raluca's time to work with the team and was amazed by the results. As a result of this, the team decided to work directly with some of the users during the building of the functionality so issues could be spotted before they became an issue. This drastically reduced the number of defects later found in production.

It wasn't until the team were exposed to the experience of real users in the contact centre that they realised what a bug really was. After that experience, however, fixing it wasn't just about providing a technical solution but rather eliminating a customer problem and enabling customer value smoothly.

This brings to mind another pattern that I have noticed:

Good teams focus on the important work they are given.
Great teams help find where the important work is.

> **What would a more proactive approach to quality give you? What would it give others?**

Pick-Up Sticks

In principle, the Boy Scout Rule is a great idea. However, because of the complex nature of how the product had evolved, there were times when the Avengers ended up making things worse by fixing things immediately.

When there are a lot of dependencies within the code base teams might need to become a little more considered in their actions. For this reason, the Avengers adopted a rule called the Mikado Method [3] to map out the landscape before making a change.

The Mikado Method is named after the simple yet popular game of "pick-up sticks" which rewards patience and a logical order of working out the safe path to the desired stick (or in this case enhancement) without disrupting other sticks (or in this case features of the system). The idea is to remove one obstacle at a time in order to achieve real results without bringing down the whole "pile of sticks" and this is a good way for teams to reduce the risk of making changes in real-time.

We Don't Have a Choice

Many teams claim that they don't have the option of doing things properly. They are told that both dates and scope have been fixed so their only choice is to "do the best they can" which often translates to "get something done that looks like it works".

Of course, agile teams will be regularly building incomplete functionality as part of their iterative, incremental approach to development. Great teams, however, keep the quality bar high and instead compromise on how much functionality is present. It is easier to add functionality later than it is to recover lost quality and indeed lost customers. Often, delaying a release is the best long-term solution [Card QC4].

In these situations, when I speak to the people who are supposedly putting these constraints in place and not allowing the team to maintain quality standards, their main driver is a concern that the team wants to gold-plate everything and indulge in unnecessary intricacies that won't justify the cost when customers are waiting for deliveries.

Both parties here have valid concerns and it is easy to see how a "them and us" state can develop, but if the focus is on "beating" the other party then, in reality, both sides lose. The main issue here is the lack of an open, humble, empathic, trusting conversation about quality.

> *What indicators are there that you might have the balance of quality and delivery wrong?*

Great teams start that conversation and accept they have a responsibility for building quality into their work. They also acknowledge how difficult things are for product owners and management who are trying to delight or at least satisfy the customers and users, and help them understand how a little extra time spent doing things right will pay off for them with interest in the medium to long term.

Great teams also know that once compromises are made on quality, it is very hard to stop the integrity of the product from getting progressively worse because that "debt" becomes more like compound interest. Problems don't add up linearly; they add up exponentially [4]. Once the integrity of the product is slipping, team morale and customer satisfaction inevitably follow.

Great teams take a stand for quality [Card QC5] and have a professional pride about what they deliver. They constantly strive to hit "bug zero" – that state where the product is perfectly free from defects and all users are not only satisfied but delighted. [Card QC6]

Hitting "bug zero" is not a prerequisite of greatness. Great teams don't need to achieve perfection, but that does not stop them from constantly working towards it. They become perfectly imperfect [Card QC7].

This process can take time and great teams are patient in their pursuit of excellence. So long as their quality bar is inching higher, they will be satisfied. Just as we mentioned in the Self-Improvement section, marginal gains can be just as dramatic as big leaps, and progress is what keeps great teams going.

When Are We "Done"?

One simple technique that great teams tend to use in order to push themselves forward in this area is the continuous and ruthless focus on extending their definition of "done". The term "done" is important to teams building a product iteratively for many reasons, not least of which because it helps everyone understand the degree to which the product is expected to be functional.

For example, in month six of a project, the team may consider "done" to mean "delivered to users for testing in the staging environment"; however, in month nine, "done" could be enhanced to mean "signed off by users in the staging environment". What is the value in this? Well, any issues found in month six will take a lot longer to fix and have a bigger impact on current development than they would if the definition of "done" was the same as in month nine.

Often, a team are required to constrain their definition of "done" because of limitations placed on them by their environment, skillset or external dependencies. This is OK, because the team are still doing the best they can, but it will feel frustrating to them and, if we are being brutal, the organisation will not feel any benefit because it is only when something is "done" that value is realised.

In situations like this, great teams acknowledge the limitations of their context but don't accept them. Great teams do not shirk responsibility; instead they will constantly chip away at what is within their control and work on creating compelling cases for those with influence to help change the context to make quality improvements easier.

Over time, a team will notice many aspects of the work that could be added to the definition of "done" to avoid replicating the issue in the future. As they get closer to Team Mastery, however, a great team will take the proactive steps of routinely reviewing the definition for improvement opportunities.

SUMMARY

Great teams:

- Empathise with their customers and users
- Take a proactive, whole-team approach to quality
- Know that not all aspects of quality are visible or predictable
- Aim for excellence in the pursuit of ever-elusive perfection
- Continuously inspect and adapt their definition of "done"

TRY THIS:

*Ask a cross-section of people to rate the
quality levels of your product*

| *Far too many bugs* | *Slightly too many bugs* | *Perfect balance* | *Slightly over-engineered* | *Way too over-engineered* |

The team in the last story had a strong sense of intrinsic motivation when it came to quality. It was important to them, personally, that they built something of high quality. That is a common trend of great teams and an ever-more commonly observed facet of motivation in today's complex world.

Quality in an agile team is a whole-team responsibility. I am not just responsible for "doing my bit right" but ensuring that we, as a team, have built something with integrity. There is a concern that with collective responsibility comes zero responsibility, that if there isn't a single person held accountable then nobody will take accountability. However, the extra transparency that comes with an agile approach – a requirement to deliver something tangible every couple of weeks – means there is always a spotlight on the team.

Assuming a wider sense of quality requires courage. It feels safer to stay with what we know; safer to keep doing what we have always done. Yet, nowadays this is a false security. As a species, we are risk averse and loss averse [5] so, given the choice, we will typically keep what we have. This, though, is at odds with the world the majority of the workforce finds themselves in.

My father-in-law worked very hard. He left school at fifteen with "two O-Levels and a cycling proficiency certificate" as he will happily tell anyone who will listen. Yet he successfully worked his way up through a large building society to eventually become a director. He worked for one company his entire working life and the purpose (and structure) of that organisation didn't fundamentally change during his career. I worked at BT, a company that had a history of people joining at sixteen and staying there their whole career ... a job for life.

This is not an option for my children ... it was barely an option for me. Industries, organisations and even teams and individuals are subject to such rapid and frequent change that the average lifespan of a large organisation is less than 20 years (compared to 60 years in 1958) [6] so it is almost guaranteed that your career will outlast your employer.

There are still situations where cause and effect can be determined in advance; where repeatability and efficiencies are the right things to aim for. But, in more and more industries, domains and organisations, quality these days involves widening one's skill base to remain adaptable and relevant; it requires us to be open to the unknown, the changing and the complexities in our organisations, because quality is rarely known upfront.

In these complex domains, we need to start work with incomplete information and, as crazy as it might sound, be prepared to "reinvent the wheel". Over the years, the wheel has been reinvented multiple times with great results, often to get past the need for wheels. In these environments, we need to move our quality focus away from efficiency in order to be effective.

The classic differentiation between efficiency and effectiveness is that "efficiency is doing the thing right while effectiveness is doing the right thing". As you can see, they are both valuable in the right context.

Efficiency is great because it involves an optimisation of a process through the minimisation of wasted resource. Efficiency leads to great returns on our investment because it provides maximum output for minimal input. It is only really possible to focus on efficiency, however, when there is stability, predictability and repeatability. When there is high volatility, it is impossible to standardise enough to make a process efficient.

Effectiveness, on the other hand, involves the letting go of an efficient way of doing things and often involves responding in the moment to be successful. In an unpredictable environment, it is much more important for us to be constantly looking at whether we are doing the right thing than worrying about doing it efficiently.

People these days find themselves working in cross-functional teams; a group of people with different disciplines to their own rather than working in a silo of people with a similar skillset. They find themselves required to work outside of a rigid job description and do the work that is needed rather than the work they are typically qualified to do.

Broadening one's skillset and delivering in an agile way as part of a cross-functional team involves "the F word": failure.

Rarely has one seven-letter word carried as much stigma. We go out of our way to avoid failure – and this is, in many ways, a great thing. However, in the world of unknown unknowns, it is impossible to prevent all possible failures and so great teams find ways to reduce the fear and stigma of failure, allow room for inevitable failure and, even better, to learn from it.

The following story illustrates this well as Claire, Kirk, Michaela and Emilio are undergoing some training with Lee, to help them respond to the unpredictable while preparing for the preventable.

Fail To Succeed

A good team prepares for the preventable.
A great team develops resilience for the unpredictable.

"Sixty-five-year-old female, in a car accident thirty minutes ago, unresponsive at the scene, severe bruising to the chest and in acute pain with a broken leg," said Lee, loud enough to be heard above the screaming coming from the corridor. "Claire … you're up; everyone else, grab a hat."

Taken a little by surprise, Claire took the team leader hat and everyone else took a different hat with a letter on as the patient was wheeled in.

"MY LEG! MY LEG!" shouted the lady on the stretcher, clearly in agony.

Everyone could see the bone protruding from the skin – a clear compound fracture – as well as the cuts to her face and her bloodstained clothes.

Claire seemed a little overwhelmed for a second before gathering herself and getting to work.

"Her airway is fine but get her neck stable, Kirk," she said, assertively, before asking the patient to confirm her name and telling her that they had her situation under control.

"OK June, we are going to give you something for the pain and then sort your leg, OK?" Claire said.

"Neck stabilised," said Kirk.

"Great job. OK, Michaela get her some morphine and Emilio can reset the leg," said Claire.

Michaela and Emilio sprang into action, but before any morphine could be given, June took a turn for the worse.

"She's turning blue, Claire, and her heart rate is rising," said Lee.

Claire panicked and instructed Emilio to perform CPR. Emilio looked apprehensive but followed Claire's instructions. One minute later and Lee told everyone to stop and announced that the patient had died. The team looked crestfallen.

"Thank you, June. You can go and grab a coffee," Lee said.

June, an actress, sat up and gave Claire a smile that said "nice try but better luck next time" before getting down and leaving the room.

Lee is an Advanced Trauma Life Support (ATLS) trainer running an open day for Claire and the rest of her team. He quickly led a debrief.

"You got attracted by the obvious broken leg and the cries of pain took your attention away from the more serious problem. So despite the fact that she was in cardiac arrest, she had a punctured lung which CPR would not fix. This is why we follow the Primary Survey process."

The Primary Survey that Lee was referring to is an international standard for triaging trauma patients in order to ensure that the trauma team address the most life-threatening injuries first.

"You were biased by the information you received from the paramedic and the patient," Lee explained. "Regardless of the presenting information, you must remain neutral and follow the ABCDE model. You jumped from Airway (A) to Environment (E) missing out on Breathing (B), Circulation (C) and Disability (D), so the patient died.

"Everyone get ready to take a new hat; the next patient will be arriving in five minutes. This time, Emilio, you will be team lead."

At the end of the day, the team were exhausted but they had loved it. They gradually got better at triaging and rotated their roles so much that everyone got a chance to give and receive orders from each other.

They had begun to internalise a new muscle memory for assessing situations on their merits and prioritising their analysis in a crisis situation. While this was predominantly a team-building event, when they were discussing the day over dinner that evening, they all thought the lessons learned could be applied to their own work environment. They liked the idea of preparing for the worst [Card QC8].

"Not only would it be really useful to do some disaster planning for what we do but simulating it would actually be really fun and a great way to prepare ourselves to think calmly in a crisis situation. It could also be a great way of onboarding new people and bringing them up to speed on how we work," said Emilio.

"I agree," said Michaela, "and I've already got some ideas for some scenarios."

When the team got back to the office, they immediately pitched the idea of creating some simulated disaster recovery scenarios – provisionally titled War Games – to management, who loved the idea in principle, but took some convincing about the risk and disruption they felt it might cause.

Claire and the team agreed to draw up some principles of the War Games process to clarify things for them and for management. They created a poster which they stuck on the wall and they also created, with the help of management, a small database of previous incidents that they would turn into training scenarios.

WAR GAMES

- BASED ON REAL SCENARIOS
- PLAY IT OUT AS REAL
- NO DISRUPTION TO PRODUCTION
- ROTATE THE ROLES
- DEBRIEF IMMEDIATELY
- DOCUMENT IT ALL
- EVERY OTHER FRIDAY AFTERNOON
- EXPECT THE UNEXPECTED
- STABILISE THE PATIENT

Everyone on the team agreed to take turns adopting different roles within the War Games scenarios and got agreement from account managers and the Product Owner to invest that time every fortnight. It was easily rationalised and the benefits were felt very quickly, most notably their ability to respond to outages quickly and effectively. The team's mean time to recovery improved from over a day to under an hour. This meant that any outage was fixed within sixty minutes.

"In theory, there is no difference between theory and practice, while in practice there is."

Benjamin Brewster

A simple risk mitigation exercise is good practice for many teams, but, in my experience, this all-too-often stops at a hypothetical discussion of the most obvious risks.

In the heat of the moment, it is often difficult to recall our training unless we have practised our skills under pressure. Hence, the trauma team and the War Games are practised regularly and in as near real-life scenarios as possible. This allows us to normalise the crisis and think more calmly about the unpredictable.

> *What might happen that could create*
> *a crisis for us as a team?*

The 3F Instinct

Preparation and rehearsal allow people to respond more rationally to a crisis. If we are unprepared for something dramatic then there is a good chance that our primal instincts will kick in – what is often referred to as the fight or flight instinct. There is actually a third, often overlooked element to this, which is where we neither face down a threat nor run away from it; instead we simply freeze and do nothing. I call it the "3F instinct".

In prehistoric times, this instinct was very useful a lot of the time. Our field of vision narrows (literally) so our attention is focused on what is directly in front of us and not distracted by the periphery. These days, however, the ability to think calmly and creatively is more useful to us than the 3F instinct and so finding ways to bypass this instinct could be valuable to us as individuals and teams.

Normalisation of the Scary

One way of bypassing the 3F instinct is to normalise the scary. The more we become accustomed to the unknown and the threatening, the less of an instinctive response it generates within us and the more rational we can be about it. This is why great teams do not shy away from their fears but rather face them in safe situations.

Sports teams will practise match situations that are likely to be difficult to process so that they have a plan for how to act if and when it arrives. Medical teams will prepare for emergencies so that they are able to adopt a wider field of vision when the situation demands it.

Fear is a huge part of individual and team development, and there are many books, courses and coaches who can help you with specific fears, but there are also some techniques that you can apply to most situations that can help almost anyone.

The first is contextualising the fear and this starts with applying a little cold logic to the situation. For example, most people are not dealing with life or death situations and so, when put into the context of "What's the worst that could ACTUALLY happen here?", we can turn the dial down from ten to maybe an eight or a seven.

The second technique that I have found amazingly helpful to almost every individual and team that I have worked with is "fear-setting". I adapted this from a TED talk by Tim Ferris [7] and it is beautifully simple.

Fear-Setting

It starts by listing the fears associated with a situation or a potential course of action. Just getting them out of your head and onto paper. This is often an eye-opening step because the longer things stay in your head, the more they tend to appear inflated and dramatic but so often the first response people have to this first step is "Oh, there aren't that many actually".

Then, for each of the fears you have listed, try and think of some way that you can "reduce it", "repair it" and "reframe it".

TAKING OWNERSHIP AS A TEAM OF A DECISION THAT WE WOULD USUALLY ESCALATE TO MANAGEMENT

CONCERN	REDUCE	REPAIR	REFRAME
MANAGEMENT MAY FEEL UNDERMINED AND THREATENED	IF WE DO A THOROUGH RISK PLAN AND PREPARE A LOGICAL EXPLANATION, THEY WILL SEE IT WAS THOUGHT THROUGH	WE COULD APOLOGISE, SHOW CONTRITION AND EXPLAIN WHAT WE LEARNED FROM THE EXPERIENCE	MANAGEMENT MIGHT REALISE THERE IS A NEED FOR AUTONOMY AND TRAINING
WE MAY GET SACKED	IF WE MITIGATE THE BIG RISKS, ANY FAILURE WILL BE LESSENED AND WE COULD TRY MULTIPLE THINGS IN PARALLEL SO ONE OF THEM MIGHT WORK	WE COULD DEVELOP A ROLL-BACK PLAN SO SHOULD IT NOT WORK OUT THEN WE COULD REVERT TO HOW IT WAS BEFORE	IF WE GET SACKED FOR MAKING A THOUGHT-THROUGH DECISION, WE MAY REALISE THIS ISN'T THE WORK PLACE FOR US
WE MAY GET IT WRONG AND CAUSE PROBLEMS	BY APPLYING OUR LOGIC AND EXPERIENCE, PLUS SEEKING ADVICE FROM OTHER EXPERTS WE CAN REDUCE THE CHANCES	WE COULD EXPLAIN THAT "NO ACTION" WOULD HAVE BEEN EVEN WORSE	THIS COULD BE A GOOD OPPORTUNITY TO TALK ABOUT HOW MUCH RISK THERE IS IN OUR PROCESSES

For example, if I am worried about taking ownership of a decision that normally gets escalated to management then I would start by listing the specific consequences that I am worried about as a result of taking this action.

I may, for example, be concerned that management feel undermined and will thus make my life difficult; I may be worried that I will get sacked or make a mistake that causes problems for the users.

Taking each of these concerns in turn, I would attempt to identify ways to reduce either the chances of that concern becoming a reality or the scale of its impact, then ways I could repair the situation should it become a reality before finally taking an alternative perspective and reframing it as a potential benefit.

The first benefit of fear-setting is that most teams find very few specific concerns when they try to list them. Just getting the fear out of their heads and onto paper often clarifies how much the fear has escalated in their minds. Then, by creating a prevention plan and a recovery plan they feel much more comfortable tackling the fear before considering how even "failure" could be beneficial to them.

> *What could you have been overly*
> *worrying about as a team?*

Don't Panic, Pick Your Process

Taking inspiration from the Cynefin Framework [8], there are different types of responses that are appropriate in different circumstances. Procedures should be followed for anything that best practice has been established for. In the case of the trauma team, decades of experience has shown a prioritised list of checks to be performed. This should be followed without thinking.

When things become more complicated, and there is no obvious procedure to follow, we should act based on principles. To return to the trauma team, once a patient has been stabilised, the team will gather data from scans and medical history to fill out the picture and find out logically which direction to follow next. When things are relatively predictable, analysis and preparation is a very efficient and effective use of time.

When the future is less predictable though, time spent analysing and preparing is more likely to be wasted effort and, in those situations, energy is better spent creating options and preparing to respond to what comes our way. If our patient remains unstable then probing based on clinical priorities and responding to what we discover makes more sense than rigid adherence to processes.

If things are too unstable and bordering on chaos then almost any decision is better than none. If we don't have the data to make an analytical decision or the time to probe, then a trauma team will make a decision to try something knowing that inaction is likely to cause death. Of course, action could also lead to death but they can sleep at night knowing that they did something because any action in a matter of life or death will, at the very least, give the patient a chance and give us data to work with.

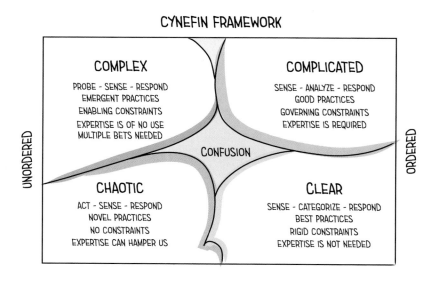

The Cynefin Framework © Cognitive Edge [8]

Of course, most teams are not dealing with life or death situations on a daily basis, but the principles of situational awareness and contextual decisiveness coupled with mindful reflection are key to all teams striving for Team Mastery.

Not all decisions will work out perfectly, certainly not in complex domains, and acknowledging this will help avoid paralysis. It is very easy for teams to fear the consequences of a wrong decision and use this fear to do an appropriate amount of due diligence where that is useful. However, great teams also realise there is a limit to this and will not allow a fear of consequences to stop them from being decisive when that is the right thing to do. [Card AC3]

As well as simply asking ourselves "What's the worst that can happen?", another way that great teams reduce the fear associated with a decision is to pare it right back to the simplest state. This is a good practice when it comes to the working process as well. The best way to find bottlenecks and issues in the lifecycle is to reduce the batch size to one and process single-piece flow [Card QC9].

Great teams also have a resilience about them, not just from greater coverage within their ranks and overlap of skills and experience, but also a sense of "bounceback*agility*" – a term I have come up with [Card QC10].

The term "bounceback*ability*" was coined by football manager Iain Dowie [10] to refer to his team's ability to respond positively to defeat. Agile teams know that, like sports teams, setbacks are both inevitable and not final. In many cases, exerting energy to prevent failure hits the law of diminishing returns and instead channelling that energy into being able to learn from, and positively respond to, failure is more useful.

Good teams will do whatever they can to avoid mistakes from being made and there is huge value in that; but great teams step out of their comfort zone and realise that some events cannot be planned for and, instead, attempt to learn as quickly as possible then respond to what they discover.

The stepping outside of one's comfort zone requires an environment of "psychological safety", a state defined by Kahn [11] as "being able to show and employ one's self without fear of negative consequences of self-image, status or career".

There are four patterns that I have seen great teams adopt to increase their sense of psychological safety for making decisions that could become seen as "mistakes". These patterns also help develop their bouncebackagility.

The first pattern is defining good mistakes. When faced with the prospect of unknown unknowns, great teams plan to make good mistakes and to take energy from them rather than become demotivated by things not working out perfectly. A good mistake [12] is one that:

- is made in good faith;
- is made in the pursuit of doing the right thing rather than the fear of making the wrong decision;
- allows us to find out what works and what doesn't work quickly and cheaply;
- keeps as many options open as possible for as long as possible;
- reduces risks early.

What might a "good mistake" look like for you?

The second pattern is to *decide as a team*. By taking a collective stand, we feel less vulnerable individually, so assessing options and looking at multiple perspectives then taking a stance as a team increases our ability to make a mistake and then recover from it as a team.

The third pattern that great teams adopt is to focus on the decision not the outcome. As Annie Duke points out in her book *Thinking In Bets* [12], great teams know that a negative outcome does not necessarily mean it was a bad decision. Great teams can bounce back quicker when they can rationalise the decision was sound even if the result was not what they wanted.

The fourth and final pattern that great teams employ is to make lots of small bets, often in parallel. Rather than put "all their eggs in one basket", great teams try many small bets and see which one emerges as the best. This stops things from becoming a coin-flip, win or lose scenario and increases the chances for ultimate success.

SUMMARY

Great teams:

• Treat quality as a whole-team responsibility
• Plan to avoid catastrophic "bad mistakes"
• Define what they mean by "good mistakes" and aim for them
• Develop their bouncebackagility
• Make lots of small bets when facing uncertainty

TRY THIS:

Identify a worst case scenario that could completely derail your team. Create a simulation then practice dealing with it so you are confident should it ever occur.

SQUAD

Unity

"Coming together is a beginning.
Keeping together is progress.
Working together is success."

Henry Ford

Unity

We all know that teams are more than just groups of people put together for a piece of work or who just happen to sit together or find themselves in the same department.

There are many definitions of what makes a team a team, but a sense of togetherness, a common goal, a sense of camaraderie or what I tend to call "unity" would never be argued against. Find me a great team that aren't united and I will eat my proverbial hat. Indeed, great teams stop becoming great as soon as disunity sets in.

A united team not only leads to greater productivity and an increased chance of experiencing "flow" [1] but also increases the resilience and even pain-tolerance of each individual member!

A study of Oxford university rowers found that those exercising in team formation could last much longer than when rowing alone. This fact, coupled with the fact that people are less likely to give up [2] when in a team and a united team often produces more than the sum of its individual parts, proves how important a sense of unity is to the individuals and the organisation itself.

A sense of belonging is one of the core needs of human beings in almost all models of human needs from Tony Robbins [3] to the Human Givens [4] to Maslow's Hierarchy of Needs [5]. Knowing that we are accepted as part of a "tribe", and can rely on others, increases our sense of security and happiness. We are, after all, social beings. This fact is even more important when operating in what Cynefin theory would call complex or chaotic environments because anxiety is heightened when humans feel less in control and in a less-predictable state.

One way of developing a sense of unity is to ensure that the team have a common goal to rally around and towards; a sense of purpose.

Great teams not only know what they are attempting to achieve but can map their identity to that goal as well.

In the following story, Product Owner Zara gives the Call of Duty team a clear sense of customer purpose for their next piece of work, but Frederick, Tony, Spencer and the rest of the team realise that sometimes a team can be too aligned to the customer, so craft their identity as a team to help them become great.

Who Do We Think We Are?

A good team unites around a goal.
A great team unites around an identity.

"Are you sitting comfortably? Then I'll begin," Zara the Product Owner said as the Call of Duty team settled into their chairs. They were preparing to review a new feature they had just developed for the company's investment product.

"Once upon a time, there was a self-employed graphic designer called Xiao," Zara continued, pointing to a picture of a smiling, twenty-something she had printed off and stuck to the wall.

"And every day, Xiao would work for multiple demanding clients creating amazing artwork that was featured in marketing campaigns and product pitches. Her work was appreciated but nobody was really aware how much time she spent perfecting her artwork. She loved her job and wanted everything to be perfect."

Zara showed a couple of examples of Xiao's work, which the team were impressed by.

"As well as worrying about losing her current clients, with the market for her skills being very competitive, Xiao also worried about the future because, as a self-employed artist, she had no company pension plan, so she saved as much as she could every month into an account with poor returns."

Members of the team could empathise with that!

"Until one day," Zara continued, with dramatic emphasis, "Xiao heard about a new type of investment that attracted significant tax relief and offered the potential of not stellar, but decent returns. Xiao was nervous. Was it too good to be true? Could she afford to take the risk and do something different than what she had always done?"

Zara showed a mock-up of an advert for the company's new flagship investment product Lorem Ipsum, designed to appeal to people like Xiao.

"She decided that, because there was no minimum investment, she could start with a small investment and minimise her risk. She got reports to show her how things were progressing and read favourable news reports about the company and the product and, because of that, decided to switch more of her savings into Lorem Ipsum. Until finally, Lorem Ipsum was Xiao's only place for savings and she worried less about the future."

The team were buzzing about this. They loved the opportunity to build something that they could identify with and, even more so when they could empathise and connect with the people who would be using the product. Zara knew from past experience that having clear goals helped to excite the team and inspire their creativity.

The team started talking about the user journeys that would be built to make this a reality for Xiao. They broke it up into big chunks of functionality and decided to split off into pairs to brainstorm more details for a timebox of fifteen minutes before coming back as a group.

After the fifteen minutes were up, the whole team reconvened with bunches of sticky notes that each pair played back to the rest of the team, explaining the user journeys they had sketched out.

Most of the user journeys were fairly straightforward and only increased the level of excitement within the team. The team got so engaged that they even suggested the creation of a "bundled product" that would give the user both an investment opportunity and a form of insurance.

When the team pitched the bundled product to Zara, however, she didn't seem anywhere near as keen as they did.

"Hmmm. I love your creativity but it's not possible I'm afraid," said Zara. "The regulator would kill us if we did this."

"But Xiao would LOVE this. WE would love this!" Frederick, one of the new members of the team, implored.

"I'm sure she would. But the customer is just one persona to consider here. There are new regulations and the fine for breaking them would be share-price affecting," Zara replied.

"Wow," said Tony, one of the developers, "we definitely do NOT want to get into trouble with the regulator, so I guess we have to rethink it. Would you be able to explain the new regulations to us so we can learn a bit more about the context we are operating in, please?"

"Absolutely," Zara said. "In fact, I've written something from the perspective of a regulator's persona."

Zara talked the team through the perspective of the regulator and handed out copies of the new regulations that were relevant to the product.

After the team had asked a few clarifying questions, Zara went on, "I mentioned in our last appreciations session [Card UC1] that I love how much you focus on the customer but we all need to be careful we don't neglect the other main stakeholders. The regulator and the shareholders are really important to this product's success too."

"We've always had customer centricity as an important part of our team identity," Tony said to Frederick and the rest of the team, "but Zara is right. We should remember that Xiao is not the only stakeholder here and WE are not the customer."

How do Teams Get an Identity?

Tony was referring to an exercise that one of the team members, Spencer, led them through a few months before. When Frederick joined the team, they decided it would be a good opportunity to get together and meet each other, some of them for the first time [Card UC2].

Most of the team had been working together for a while but they were not all based in the same location and didn't see each other often. Recently, there had been a couple of awkward situations that had been difficult for them to resolve as a team. A few team members had different ideas for what to do, but there was no real way to decide, so Spencer explained an exercise he did with a team at his previous company that really helped them create an identity as a team.

There are countless ways for teams to create their identity but, often, the easiest way is through stories and values. Capturing and sharing stories of their past personal experiences that showcase examples of desirable and undesirable actions, makes it much easier to relate, remember and reinforce as a team.

Spencer gave every member of the team a pack of large sticky notes and asked them to consider three fictional yet realistic customer experience scenarios, one at a time. For each of the scenarios, he asked each team member to write down how a team could respond in a way that (a) would leave them proud; (b) would leave them comfortable; (c) they could tolerate but would be a little uncomfortable with; and (d) they would veto.

They did this in silence. Then the responses were grouped and the team were asked to reflect on the responses and use them to begin crafting a team identity. That identity would capture how they would like to act as a team in general, using those scenarios as examples.

Why is an Identity Important?

After the Call of Duty team had crafted an identity, they found that deciding how to tackle specific situations became a lot easier and everyone had a much better idea of what was expected of them, what was acceptable and what was not.

During the identity exercise, for example, Frederick, Tony and Spencer all found out that they had a strong sense of fairness and integrity in their personal identity and felt that this, coupled with a desire for providing good service and delighting customers, meant that they could all agree on how they would like to act when facing conflicting demands.

When they reflected on this exercise, the team found great value from finding out about one another [Card UC3]. They described feeling less tension and noticed fewer passive-aggressive comments. Team members cited how much more productive they were because they needed to spend less time second-guessing how to act because they could look back to that team identity and just "know" what to do.

All great teams have an identity; they know what they stand for and what they will not stand for. They have a common and clear understanding of what they expect from one another without having to detail the specific expectations of every situation. It's like a code that binds the team members together to something bigger than themselves and it makes it much easier to trust one another – a mandatory factor of great teams [Card UC4].

Another powerful factor in creating strong team bonds is symbolism. Many great sports teams cite how important "the badge" or "the jersey" or "the club" is to their motivation and sense of purpose. The great agile teams I have witnessed leverage this aspect of symbolism too. From team t-shirts to team logos, from team coffee mugs to team rituals; great teams create a sense of "us" and are proud to show that off.

> *What is "something bigger" that could bind*
> *you together as a team?*

A regulated industry is a good example of a common situation that product development teams find themselves in where they are being pulled in different directions by competing stakeholders.

In the illustration below, the three competing stakeholders are: the customers, the shareholders and the regulator. These stakeholders have different, and often conflicting, goals and drivers. The customers want functionality and speed; the shareholders want profit and reputation; the regulator wants standards and fairness.

The Stakeholder Triangle

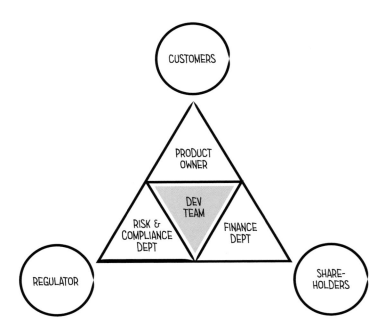

Most organisations have internal people or departments to manage these stakeholders and represent their needs. Often, a Product Owner will represent the customers, the finance department will represent the shareholders, and the risk and compliance department will represent the regulator. This often leaves the product development team in the middle either being squashed or pulled apart by these competing and often seemingly irreconcilable demands.

Team unity is important in such situations because competing stakeholders can easily create unhelpful friction between team members. It is almost impossible for a team to avoid aligning more to the customer than the other stakeholders, because customer happiness is a highly motivating factor.

On the face of it, this has to be a good thing, right? How many times have you heard "We should be more customer-centric" or wished that a company cared more about what you – as a customer – wanted, thought or felt?

Indeed, in this story, the Call of Duty team had "Customer Centricity" as one of their core values in their team charter. Having empathy with your customers is a good thing, but great teams are aware that there is always a risk of over-identification (effectively, too much empathy).

So, while great teams are indeed very focused on the customer, they don't forget the other important stakeholders; and this holistic view is often something baked into the team identity.

Social Identity Theory

Henri Tajfel asserted in 1979 that the groups to which we belong are an important source of pride and self-esteem; they give us a sense of belonging and help define how we see ourselves. He called this Social Identity Theory [6] and he suggests that one way to increase our sense of self is to enhance the status of the group or team to which we belong. The better the team, the better we are.

Obviously, the reverse applies too, as an individual's personal sense of value can be overly damaged by being part of an under-performing team, so one needs to be careful with tying too much of our personal identity to that of others, but the upside is definitely present in all of the great teams I have witnessed.

There is another downside to Social Identity Theory and that is the "out group". The out group refers to the temptation to include defining who you are not as part of defining who you are. For example, part of seeing your team as the best can be through explaining why other teams are not good, putting down the competition if you will.

This is visible in sport (think trash-talking boxers) but also in wider society (think tribal conflicts or nationalism) and, while competition can be motivating, there is a chance that it could lead to unhelpful and even destructive behaviour.

While a great team with a strong identity can be a hugely influential force for change within the organisation, role-modelling greatness, there is the possibility of overly-strong competition across teams, undermining the organisation as a whole.

One interesting way I have seen great teams tackle this is to ensure that their identities are compatible and even themed with each other. For example, each team takes a musical band as their identity and these bands are part of a product-wide "festival". Bands are great, but festivals are awesome, and all contribute to the wider success of the business.

What if it's Broken?

Sometimes people just don't fit into the team. That doesn't make them a bad person; it doesn't even make them a bad team player. They may flourish in another team; it can simply be personal chemistry.

In general, great teams tend to assume more of the responsibility for a person "fitting in" than they place on the individual themselves. Paul Goddard writes in his book *Improv-ing Agile Teams* that the Comedy Store Players often bring guest comedians into their shows and, instead of the guest fitting into the team's existing norms and rules, the team "flex to accommodate the contrasting style that a new improviser can bring". [7]

By consciously adjusting the team's style and approach to the newcomer, the team minimises the risk of being a "closed shop" or clique that stagnates with their entrenched habits and groupthink.

If the team has tried to incorporate that individual, and that individual has tried to assimilate themselves into the team but it hasn't worked, then sometimes it is best to cut our losses and agree to a parting of ways.

This is often seen as a failure, but I believe it is an opportunity for all parties to achieve their full potential in alternative configurations. It happens.

> *What signs could you look out for to avoid your team becoming a clique?*

Models such as Tuckman's Stages of Group Development [8] and Katzenbach & Smith's Team Performance Curve [9] concur that not only does a team go through stages of development – some that feel like a backward step – but they also need to revisit their identity when the team composition changes, such as when a new team member joins. This will reduce the risk of separate sub-teams or cliques forming and open the team up to reaching new heights.

This revisiting and recontracting is important for ownership of the identity for members new and old and in "levelling the playing field" for all to feel part of the team.

Ideally teams will use a strong identity to reduce the number of instances where a team member acts "out of line", but it is unreasonable to expect that this will remain the case. Great teams handle these situations in a common way by following these key principles:

1. *Assume positive intent.* When given the choice of how to interpret someone's actions, great teams choose to assume the best, most positive option. They choose to believe that the team member in question was acting in good faith or, if this is not the case, then it was a cry for help.

2. *Face the future.* Great teams are also able to extract maximum learning and value from such experiences. Yes, they could reap some benefit from looking at what caused this situation, but great teams take the view that they will probably get more value from looking at how they can learn from it to make the future better.

As well as adopting this positive, solutions-focused mindset, great teams will happily consider asking for help [Card UC5] to re-establish unity. In fact, showing vulnerability and humility is a sign of greatness in itself. Great teams know that they cannot handle everything themselves and accept that asking for help is a sign of strength not weakness.

> *How well can you discuss and resolve a situation where the team identity is undermined?*

How Does Identity Evolve?

Over time, the identity of the team will evolve. As the capacity of the team grows and as they encounter and deal with new situations – both successfully and unsuccessfully – their identity will change slightly. The core values of the team that underpin that identity will likely remain stable, but the expectations and tolerance levels can change.

In our story above, the Call of Duty team added the phrase "We are not the customer" to their team charter and also refined one of their other values of "Fairness" to include their duty to the other stakeholders. Great teams regularly review both their identity and what behaviours are expected and unacceptable.

Just as the product is an ever-evolving entity, so developing that sense of identity for the team to self-organise within and towards is not simply a one-off activity but something that should be revisited, reinforced and refreshed continually.

SUMMARY

Great teams:

- Strive to understand the purpose behind the work
- Know what behaviours to expect of one another and hold each other to account
- Are proud of their togetherness
- Warmly welcome new ideas and people into the team
- Debate internally and support externally

TRY THIS:

Find out what values each team member holds dear and use these to craft some common team values. Every week, capture examples of living these values.

In the previous story, the team achieved a boost by getting a common agreement on what they stood for and what they were working towards. While each team's sense of unity will be unique to them, there are some common patterns that I have seen in the hundreds of teams that I have been part of and observed.

Great teams are far from perfect – there is tension and disagreement – but the ties that bind the team together more often than not outweigh the forces pulling them apart. Teams can argue and disagree and then come back together.

So, what are those ties that bind great teams together?

Commonalities

Human beings innately tend to like people who they think are like them. This is because we generally consider ourselves to be a good person and so, if someone seems similar to us we then extrapolate our positive interpretation of ourselves and project it on to the person with the similar trait or characteristic.

Contribution

Almost paradoxically, we also need to feel different, at least different enough to the others in the team to be able to feel as though we are contributing enough as ourselves. We need to feel both a valued and valuable member of the team. This is not just to do with the skills and experiences of the individuals but also team size. In a team of twenty, each individual is just five percent of the team. In a group of eight, however, each person makes a much bigger impact on the whole team.

Care

Great teams care about each other. Not just about whether they are doing their work but how they are doing as people. This is also related to team size because it is much harder to care deeply about nineteen people than it is to care deeply about seven other people.

Collective Results

Great teams pull together in the same direction and succeed or fail as a team. They don't "hang people out to dry" or "put someone on a pedestal" even if it was one person's shortcomings or heroism that made the difference. They debate internally but put on a united face to those outside the team. Everyone in the team knows that they are safe with each other.

Candidness

Great teams don't have to mince their words; they can say it how it is. They are respectful and direct with one another, knowing that it is nothing personal and everything is aimed at making the team better. This goes for successes too – there are no great fanfares needed to herald heroic wins or goals met; great teams don't need that.

Common Language

Great teams develop their own unique language that helps them understand each other and creates a deeper bond between them, as only they understand truly what they are talking about. [Card UC7]

It takes time to develop this level of unity and it is risky to attempt to accelerate the process because developing this depth of unity requires each member of the team to gradually share and learn more and more about each other. Over time, the levels of exposure and professional intimacy increase which, if done at a sensible pace, does not cause anxiety or distress.

Sharing our thoughts, fears, values and motivations will naturally make us feel vulnerable. But, after the vulnerability is reciprocated and we feel safe that our trust is not going to be betrayed, the results are fantastic. Team members realise they are all human, they are valued, understood and supported.

In the following story, we meet Aislinn, Wally, Leslie, Eva, Lindsey and Rashmi who have developed this sense of deep unity over time. We will see an example of a team that has learned a lot about one another so, not only do they know what each other is saying, but they also begin to know what each other is thinking.

Are You Thinking
What I'm Thinking?

A good team knows what each other is saying.
A great team knows what each other is thinking.

"Are you thinking what I'm thinking?" Aislinn asked.

"Let's go," replied Leslie and, almost immediately, something strange began to happen. If you were looking carefully, you might have noticed a set of movements that vaguely resembled a ballet performance. Leslie and Wally silently got up from their workstations, peeled off and walked swiftly but not urgently towards the door.

Less than a minute later, Eva and Lindsey got up from their workstations and walked to opposite ends of the office before Aislinn transferred the video call from her work laptop to her mobile phone and left for the door herself. She descended the stairs, walked out the front door of the building, crossed the road and walked down a side street before entering a coffee shop. Once inside, she walked to the back of the room where her colleagues had already secured a table and were handing out drinks, sticky notes and marker pens.

The team used to have a code word for "we need to convene outside of the office" [Card UC6] but now they just got a "sense" that they needed a conversation which should probably be held away from everyone else.

"I just knew that was going to happen!" Wally said. "It was only a matter of time before her true colours shone through."

Wally was referring to Karen – one of the business sales leads – who had apparently promised some flashy new features to a prospective client. Wally wasn't actually her real name – her real name was Eve but given that there was already an Eva in the team, she gave herself a nickname based on her love of Pixar movies.

"Hold on Miss Purple," said Rashmi from Aislinn's phone, "there might be another explanation for this. Lindsey, could you give us a yellow perspective please?"

"I don't know much yet, but from what I know of Karen I would say that the pressure of the quarterly sales targets is bound to be affecting her and I know that this client would be a huge coup not just for her but for the company," Lindsey said calmly. "It could also open up opportunities for us to build some of the new features that are currently too expensive. My only concern is whether unrealistic dates have been offered. I would like to believe that she wouldn't have done anything like that without speaking to us."

The colours the team were referring to came from a personality-type evaluation the team did a month ago. There were many models to choose from and the team weren't looking for something scientifically accurate, more of a conversation starter, and so picked a model that used colours [10] to depict who is who.

> *How well do you know "who is who"*
> *within your team?*

While the model is obviously a simplification of complex human personalities, reds like Aislinn are typically characterised by drive, control, decisiveness and competitiveness. Reds can be perceived to have a bit of a temper because they are more than happy to speak their mind and challenge the status quo.

Yellows, like Lindsey, typically take a more optimistic, cheerful and confident stance, seeing the glass as half full rather than half empty and always seeing possibilities and positive explanations. Blues, like Leslie, in contrast, typically take more of a "glass half empty" outlook. They would typically describe themselves as "realistic not naive" while others may perceive them as pessimistic or cynical. Blues are usually more analytical and detail-focused, preferring to be silently thoughtful compared to yellows who will be much more talkative.

Finally, greens, like Eva, are typically known for staying calm and rational, they are much more easy-going and tolerant, doing whatever they can to avoid or reduce conflict and keep team harmony.

When Rashmi referred to Wally as purple, this was the team's way of acknowledging that Wally identified as both red and blue – a mixture that creates purple.

Since the team had gone through this collective self-evaluation, they had found themselves better able to understand one another's natural dispositions and perspectives, which helped with communication and leveraging diverse perspectives. The assessment itself was done light-heartedly and they laughed at the over-simplification but also at how stereotypical their behaviours could be.

Nowadays it was fairly common for individuals to describe their daily state of mind as a colour. This morning, during their daily check-in protocol [11], for example, Rashmi had described herself as feeling 'somewhat ochre' before explaining that, for her, that meant a combination of yellow and red.

"That's the thing," said Wally, "I don't really think I know Karen well enough to say for sure so I tend to default to my natural state of suspicion. She does seem to be becoming much more of an important stakeholder though, so perhaps it is worth getting to know her better?"

"She did say in her email that she would like to talk about these new features," Aislinn said. "I could see if she could make it into a bit of a workshop and build that relationship a bit more?"

The rest of the team agreed and decided to hold judgement until they met up with Karen, something that Aislinn set up for early the following week.

At the beginning of the workshop, Karen thanked the team for the information they had sent her in advance.

"Even though I haven't met many of you before, it feels like I already know you because I have read your User Manuals [12]. I thought that was such a great thing to do that I felt it would be rude for me not to create one of my own for you."

The User Manuals that Karen was referring to were the result of an exercise the team did months ago when they were just beginning to work together. The intent was for them to learn a little bit about each other so they could start working together from a more positive footing. It was sparked by Wally explaining how much she hated when people were late for meetings and if there was one thing that she could wish for it would be that people would turn up on time.

Eva then suggested they capture each other's "pet peeve" – things that really annoy them – so they could try and avoid some of them as they got to learn how to work together. This list of pet peeves eventually turned into individual User Manuals – short documents that explained how that person works and how to troubleshoot common issues.

The team found that learning about one another made it much easier to play to one another's strengths and avoid unnecessarily upsetting team-mates [Card UC3]. The commonalities and care that this exercise generated was unanimously agreed to have had a positive effect on the team spirit and productivity.

Karen then introduced herself with a brief run-through of her User Manual based on the areas the rest of the team had used to create theirs.

"I hate it when people take a long time to get back to me because I like to get things sorted out rather than have loose ends hanging around. I much prefer phone calls to chat messages, texts or email, but would prefer a face-to-face chat over phone calls," Karen began. "I often refuse to attend a meeting that doesn't have an agenda and I have a tendency to think of people as rude if they get straight down to business without a little informal chat about personal circumstances."

Not Quite the Golden Rule

Good team members treat people as they themselves prefer to be treated.
Great team members treat people as those individuals prefer to be treated.

"I've been told that I can make people feel pressured into agreeing things they don't want to, but this is probably because I am a trained negotiator and my job often depends on getting people to say 'yes'. I am proud to be very competitive, although some people say they find that intimidating and I can talk really fast when I get excited or passionate and so I have been told a few times that I can be hard to understand."

Finally, Karen referred to the great caricatures that each team member had in their User Manual. "I don't usually like caricatures but I love these drawings because they exacerbate your personality traits rather than your physical characteristics like most caricatures do. I'd love for someone to do a caricature of me."

Each team member was depicted as a superhero representing the great superpower they identified with bringing to the team but also their Kryptonite – their equivalent of an Achilles' heel – the thing that could render them powerless. Referring back to the 5C model, this allowed people to understand who was contributing in what way to the collective results and also increased that sense of feeling valued for what they bring.

"Leslie is our resident artist," said Aislinn. "I'm sure she could be commissioned to create your avatar. It's kind of a rite of passage into the team."

"Sure thing," said Leslie, "and thanks for sharing all of that information about yourself. We've found this kind of thing a great way of learning what each other means when they are talking and behaving, and I think we are going to be working very closely with you over the next few months, so that will help tremendously."

> ### *What is everyone's "superpower" in the team?*

The team then began to explore the potential new client and Karen explained what had happened.

"In order to win the business ahead of the competition, it was essential that I gave them confidence in our ability to deliver quickly. We both know that the dates we talked about won't actually happen because there will be so many negotiations between now and then that there will always be slippage before we actually agree on an absolute delivery date, by which time you will have been able to do enough work to get us ahead of the curve."

"But what if we do that work and the client doesn't sign?" asked Wally.

"If you hadn't guessed already," Eva chimed in, "Wally is our resident doom-monger!"

Everyone, including Wally, laughed.

"I appreciate your concern there Wally, but it's OK because we know as a business that we want to develop these features anyway. So by getting a client this close to agreeing to pay for them will give my bosses the confidence to effectively work at risk."

"So we will get paid regardless?" asked Wally.

"You have my word," said Karen.

"That works for most of us," said Leslie, "but Wally prefers it in writing."

"And counter-signed by both your boss and the director," said Wally with a straight face, causing Karen to stop, open-mouthed, before

Wally continued. "I'm only joking! I may be the bluest member of the team but I'm not THAT bad!"

The fact that Wally was prepared to laugh at herself allowed the rest of the team to engage in this healthy level of banter. Banter is defined as "good-humoured, playful, or teasing conversation" [13] and is something that I have seen in every great team. It often involves a difficult process of trial and error as the team works out what is an appropriate level of teasing.

Teams that are able to bring in healthy levels of banter are usually also able to make work fun [Card UC8] and enjoy each other's company while delivering great work.

> *What is an acceptable level of banter within*
> *the team and what is "too much"?*

Having Fun with Language

Banter levels, as well as many other aspects of team identity, need to be revisited regularly and especially when a new person joins the team. Another example of having fun with language was during the World Cup in 1998, when the England football team built up a sense of unity within the camp by playing a game with the media and, in part, the nation watching.

As a team, they attempted to get as many song titles into their pre- and post-match interviews as possible without the media noticing [14]. While the team did not go on to win the competition, this sense of exclusivity and fun increased the unity within the camp.

In the story above, Karen is effectively being welcomed as a new member of the team and volunteers to participate in some of the team rituals, including the User Manual and avatar. Joining a team inevitably involves some trade-off of individuality in return for the sense of belonging and support that comes from being a member of a team [Card UC9].

Sometimes that individual trade-off comes in the form of vulnerability – sharing information about yourself or trusting others – while other times it comes in the form of reducing your focus on selfish personal goals to focus instead on team success.

Karen will also be introduced to the language that the team have been using. From team-specific code words to the colour-coding of their personality types and any other jargon they have been using as part of their day-to-day work.

From Language to Silence

As with the team in the story above, most great teams I have seen tend to develop their own language and find that having a sense of uniqueness in how they communicate with one another is a significant form of motivation. I have been told by these teams that it is reminiscent of being part of a secret club or a clique in the playground when they were children.

This aspect of exclusivity – being part of a club or team – tends to be a common motivational factor and excluding others is an essential part of this. We can't have our own language without others *not* being able to speak it. Having our own terminology, jargon or rituals are part of what bonds us to the group. These bonds need to be expanded to include new members of the team as membership grows of course [Card UC10] and great teams are also careful that the feeling of exclusivity does not lead to isolation, sabotage or sub-optimisation throughout the wider organisation.

Many great teams also develop a form of silent communication; where team members can know without needing to be told. There is a Japanese term *Ishin-denshin* [15] which denotes "a form of interpersonal communication through unspoken mutual understanding" and can feel a little like being able to read one another's minds. This ability develops over time and with repeated practice and exposure to one another.

Setting aside time every day to get to know each other better is a great ritual and was referenced early on in this story as the team's *daily check-in* protocol. Getting to know one another is a journey and one that should not be forced. Great teams will make this a conscious effort but will also be patient, so each individual opens themselves up at a pace comfortable for them.

Sharing our thoughts, fears, values and motivations is scary but trust can be accumulated incrementally so start small and build it up. When we get to a point of mutual vulnerability, the impact on the individuals within the team can be hugely normalising, reassuring and motivating.

SUMMARY

Great teams:

- Develop a respectful, safe and fun common language
- Learn how each other's minds work
- Know without needing to be told
- Understand where and how everyone contributes
- Put the team's goals above their individual goals

TRY THIS:

Invite someone in to be an "anthropologist" for a day and listen to the language the team uses and identify what does not need to be said.

A

SQUAD

Audacity

"Scared is what you are feeling;
brave is what you are doing."

Emma Donohue

Audacity

Bravery is not the absence of fear but the willingness to act in the face of fear.

Everyone is scared – we are born with fear.

Scientists will tell us that we are only scared of two things when we are born (loud noises and falling [1]) but we still have fear. And fear is a positive thing because it helps us avoid making catastrophic mistakes. We are naturally risk averse and this has served us incredibly well in our evolution. Assuming the worst when we heard a noise in the bushes probably helped us avoid being eaten in primitive times.

However, fear is our number one constraint when it comes to improvement. Fear of failure, fear of judgement – both internal and social – fear of loss of our current state and status are major factors that inhibit our courage to act and to change.

It is often said that human beings naturally fear change, but I don't believe this. I am a major believer that people do not fear change itself but they are naturally resistant to any change that they do not see the benefit in, change that they don't believe to be achievable or change which is imposed upon them.

When looking to coach an individual or a team towards a change, I have a mental model of what I call the "Change Equation" because I believe everyone evaluates any potential change in terms of three variables.

The Change Equation is something I believe that everyone calculates when considering taking on a challenge or embarking on a change. It is a simple equation but one that, when understood, can be consciously altered to significantly increase our chances of success.

The equation looks like this:

$$B \times P > C$$

Where:
B = the benefit to me
P = the probability of success
C = the cost to me

Let's say, for example, that I am considering getting fit. There are a number of costs to this including the financial cost of joining a gym or buying equipment, the emotional cost of getting up early to exercise and the opportunity cost of not being able to eat and drink what I want when I want to. If I can identify the costs then I may be able to proactively reduce those costs somewhat.

There will, hopefully, be benefits to me getting fit – or why would I bother?! I might live longer, I may be able to do more sport, I may reduce my health insurance premium for example. Identifying these may help me realise just how valuable this idea is to me.

Finally, we come to P. There is always a chance that whatever we attempt will not work. So even if the chances of success are 99%, simple mathematics will say that if the benefit and cost are equal then factoring the inevitable chance of failure will lead to people not going for it.

$$100 * 99\% < 100$$

There is one more problem. Even if we factor in the chance of failure and the left-hand side of the equation is larger than the right, we still might not take the chance.

Most of us are loss and risk averse, so we don't tend to take on opportunities that are only marginally likely to succeed. The endowment effect [2] suggests that we place an unnaturally high value on anything we currently own, and our status quo is such a thing. Because of this, we require a *significant* return on our risk to justify taking a gamble.

The following story is about the Jalapenos team and is a good example of how teams need to be brave not just with their work but also with their relationships. In this story, we see how team members John and Patrick were almost unable to work with one another until another team-mate, Suranne, bravely stepped up to help them work through their issues.

Embracing Candour

A good team catches their team-mates doing things wrong.
A great team catches their team-mates doing things right.

"That's it! I'm done!" said John. "I can't work with him any longer. Either he leaves the team, or I do."

John, one of the developers in the Jalapenos team, was referring to another team member, Patrick, who had worked at the company for over twenty years and held a job title that included the word "senior" – which Patrick made reference to often.

"What's he done now?" asked his colleague, Suranne, aware that this was far from the first time John had been upset by Patrick.

"Just read this!" John replied and turned his monitor so Suranne could see what he was pointing at.

Suranne read what appeared to be the code that John had been working on for the last couple of days with a number of comments from Patrick. Her reactions while reading included gasps of astonishment, giggles and the odd "ooooh".

"Tact has never been one of his strong points though, has it," she said.

"I didn't even ask him to go through my code. It's none of his business!" said John, getting angrier.

"I don't really want to get involved again, but he is part of the team," Suranne said tentatively.

"Well, I'm not going to be for much longer," replied John, as he got up to leave the room.

"John!" Suranne called, "just promise me you won't do anything about it for an hour or so? Just try and chill for a bit. In fact, will you come for a walk?"

John reluctantly agreed and they went out. After John had calmed down a little, he could see some merit in Patrick's comments but was still upset that they had been thrust upon him without being asked for, and also at the way they were untactfully worded.

Suranne offered to facilitate a conversation between the two of them, and maybe even the rest of the team, to try and find a way to work together.

"This is the last chance," said John. "If we don't work out how to stop him doing this kind of thing, I'm off … seriously!"

Suranne had received very little training in conflict resolution and, if you had asked her, she would have rated her facilitation skills as "mediocre" but, when she raised the idea with everyone in the team, they all supported her offer to facilitate a session on "advanced intra-team communication" as she put it.

She set the meeting for last thing in the afternoon and had called in a favour from a friend who worked at a nearby pub who let them use one of the rooms out back for a couple of hours. Everyone liked the idea of getting out of the office a little early, even if they were still working, and the hope was that an informal setting would help reduce any potential tensions.

She thanked everyone for coming and started off by going through a few ground rules for the meeting. She stated that everything that happened in the room would, for all intents and purposes, be "off the record" so long as the conversation didn't break any laws or the grounds of respect.

They would all agree what, if anything, would be written up in the last fifteen minutes of the session and that the aim of the session was to "explore our communication as a team with a view to taking it to an even higher level of effectiveness."

Suranne made a point of ensuring everyone agreed with the set-up and then began to say how this team was already so much better than the last team she was on in her previous organisation.

"There was so much bickering and so many snide comments that it felt like a school playground at times. To be honest, I hated working there, which was a shame because I think every single person on that team was a good person. They just didn't know how to play nicely with others in a group setting," she laughed.

"I'm quite a shy person by nature and so I know I'm not the best communicator, but one thing I really want to learn from all of you is how you think I could make my communication better," Suranne continued, before asking the team to offer her some completely honest feedback [Card AC1].

"You always beat around the bush," said Patrick, almost before anyone else had even processed that this was an actual request for feedback. "You never say what you really mean."

"Thanks Patrick. I appreciate that. What would be even more helpful is if you could give me a specific example of that so that I can log it and think about how I could have done it differently. Can you remember one?" Suranne asked.

"Hmmm," said Patrick, tilting his head and looking up to the ceiling, trying to remember, "when I asked you to let the contracts team know about the screw-up with the budgeting, you said that you would 'try and find a mutually agreeable resolution' or something. I don't know what that means and it makes me think you are not going to do anything."

"I can see how that might seem a bit vague to you and one thing I would not associate with you is being ambiguous," Suranne said, smiling. "I love that about you. I always know what you are thinking because you just come out and say it."

"What you see is what you get with me," said Patrick, sitting back in his chair and crossing his arms, "no point messing around."

"OK. I find it difficult to be as straight to the point as you Patrick, but I can give it a try if you like?" she said.

"Go for it," he said.

"Well I do love knowing your opinion but I can't help but take things a bit personally when you critique my work. I know I'm probably over-sensitive and I consciously remind myself that it's OK, but my mood does drop for a while," Suranne said, before quickly adding, "sorry."

"Fair enough, I do keep forgetting I work with some soft Southerners," he said, teasing those that were born anywhere south of Manchester – which happened to be everyone except him.

"Hey!" called out Rich, another of the developers, "I thought we were not going to break any grounds of respect. I know you're having a bit of a joke there Patrick but I don't think reinforcing stereotypes is a good thing."

"Woah ... OK ... I was just having a bit of a laugh, but I get your point Rich. No offence meant," replied Patrick.

There was a bit of tension in the room, which Suranne wanted to break quickly.

"I think what just happened there was great. I got some feedback and was then invited to give some feedback that I would normally have felt really uncomfortable about. Plus Rich managed to challenge someone else around a subjective value of respect. My old team would never have been able to do any of that," she said.

"We also highlighted that Patrick and I are very different in how we prefer to communicate, and that other people can appear very frustrating if their communication preferences are different to ours," Suranne continued.

"I've done a bit of research around feedback and there are so many models out there. They all seem a bit formulaic but some of them have helped me pluck up the courage to provide feedback to other people when I've been asked to in the past.

"Like I said, I want to learn from you how I can get better at communicating with you all and I thought that could be a way to introduce you to some of these feedback models and see what you like or dislike about them," Suranne said.

The team said they were interested in hearing about these models and Suranne introduced them to the AID model [3], the Perfection Game [4], the SBI model [5] and the BEEF model [6] before asking everyone about their bad experiences of receiving feedback.

As a team, they quickly compiled a list of what they called "feedback traps" – things that they hated people doing when giving them feedback. They seemed to enjoy this part of the session the most!

Feedback Traps

The Praise Sandwich – starting off with something nice, then telling them what you really want to tell them before ending with something else nice.

Inflicted Feedback – feedback that was not requested or expected but rather dumped on someone unwittingly. John enthusiastically put this one forward but others, including Patrick surprisingly, agreed.

Hints and Indirection – as Patrick said, "If I smell then just tell me. Don't leave a can of deodorant on my desk and hope I get the message!"

The Wind Up – where someone takes a long time to get to the point but you know it's coming.

Labels – attributing an occasional behaviour to their personality or character. For example, my son may have displayed an example of naughty behaviour but that does not make him a naughty boy.

Absolutes – using extreme language "You're always late" or "You never document stuff properly". It is rare for someone to be so consistent – even consistently bad!

What traps do you fall into when giving feedback
to your team-mates?

At this last one, Patrick held his hand up and said, "I did that with you Suranne when I said that you never say what you mean. My bad. I didn't mean it like that."

"That's OK Patrick. If I hadn't done the research, I may have been offended but I learned how common it was so …," Suranne replied, before adding, "but that reminds me actually. Another thing that could help me is if you could find an example of when I don't do the thing that annoys you. Finding the exception to the general rule could give me some clues about why I find it easier in some situations. And this could help me do more of it."

"That makes sense," John added, "and if we agree on something I want to get better at, you could even let me know when you notice me doing it well?"

"Yeah, kind of like catching you doing good," Suranne suggested. "That can be really powerful, a positive reinforcer."

"OK," said Patrick. "So, to be fair, you were really straight forward in our last planning session when you told that sales manager, Clinton, he couldn't just bypass the prioritisation process with his feature request. I thought you handled that really well, Suranne, because you were quite clear but still nice enough so Clinton didn't get annoyed."

"Thanks Patrick. That helps because now I have an example of something that I can perhaps do more of," Suranne responded.

The team agreed that getting better at communicating with one another would not only increase their personal happiness levels but also reduce misunderstandings and lead to better decisions and better work. They then agreed to practise giving some balanced feedback to each other on their communication style using one of the models Suranne introduced.

John and Patrick had an amicable discussion where Patrick agreed to offer his feedback only when requested and in a more constructive manner, while John agreed to take his feedback in the positive manner that it was intended.

After that, each member of the team shared one thing that they wanted to get better at over the next two weeks and gave everyone explicit permission to point out when they slipped up and also invited them to point out when they were successful. Even Maddie, the quietest member of the team, got involved, citing the structure of the feedback as helpful to her. This was a side-benefit but certainly an important one because great teams find ways to ensure everyone in the team feels comfortable to participate [Card AC2].

> *What could you invite your team-mates to give you feedback on that would help you become more effective at what you do and how you do it?*

At the end of the two weeks, the team reflected on their communication improvement and decided to take it to another level yet again. John suggested they experiment with Kudo Cards [7] to offer more public recognition of team-mates' efforts, even extending their appreciations to people outside the team, and this had a ripple effect throughout the organisation as other teams picked up on the practice.

An example of a Kudo Card

In this story, Suranne took a brave step to facilitate a session around communication and her natural facilitation skills helped a lot when it came to achieving such a successful outcome. Many teams will require a neutral facilitator from outside of the team to have these types of conversations for the first time and that's OK.

Good teams do not shy away from telling each other the truth about individual and team performance. They learn not to "beat around the bush" either, they are open and honest about their views. They are able to separate observations from judgement and deliver their messages in a respectful way so the team can use constructive feedback to improve.

Great teams also take time to build on strengths and reinforce the positive aspects of team performance that can often get overlooked. That's not to say they ignore the areas for improvement but they don't take for granted the good stuff and realise that a strength in one area, once acknowledged and appreciated, could easily be applied to other areas.

> *What good things do your team-mates*
> *do that go unrecognised?*

As well as giving feedback, great teams invite feedback from those around them, not least of whom, their users. They get to know their users and what they need, what drives them, what motivates them and take pride in using the feedback they receive to not just satisfy them but delight them. You might even say:

A good team knows their users.
A great team delights their users.

And, while this isn't always easy, we will cover that in our very next story.

SUMMARY

Great teams:

- Are scared of failure but act anyway
- Give each other honest, yet respectful, feedback
- Seek feedback from one another
- Consider other people's preferences for receiving feedback
- Will bring in neutral facilitators when necessary

TRY THIS:

Ask everyone in the team to rate how open and honest they feel they can be in their feedback to each other. Then ask what would need to happen for them to feel more comfortable.

Operating within a very traditional organisational structure while trying to work in a new way is a big challenge. It requires challenging culture, structures, policies and habits.

For example, in order to get work truly **done**, traditional team or departmental boundaries may need to be challenged or changed; lines of management may become blurred and individual incentives and rewards may need to be tweaked to encourage greater team focus.

Many people will not want to see things changed as they personally stand to benefit from the status quo. It is very easy for teams in such a situation to bow to the pressure of "that's the way we do things around here" or "respect my authority and do it this way". This is why great teams require audacity.

Great teams are not arrogant or deliberately provocative though and they respect that no person, procedure or policy is deliberately there to sabotage the success of the organisation or the team. While they are realistic enough to realise they need help, they do not sit back and expect other people to change things for them.

Great teams will, however, be prepared to be a force for change. They will act collectively for the greater good and audaciously challenge the status quo to help create a more appropriate structure to cope with the challenges of the market it finds itself in now – a market with more fierce competition, greater complexity and more volatile change.

When faced with challenge or conflict, people react differently and members of great teams learn to understand how they and others respond. The Thomas Kilmann Conflict Mode Instrument (TKI) [8] is a model that helps explain such different reactions and maps two dimensions of behaviour (assertiveness and cooperativeness) against each other.

After this mapping, the TKI defines five modes of responding to conflict:

Competing is an assertive and uncooperative response whereby an individual typically pursues their own concerns at the expense of the other person's.

The **accommodating** mode is one of unassertive cooperation and, as such, is the complete opposite of competing. When accommodating, an individual puts the concerns of the other person first, to the detriment of their own.

Avoiding is unassertive and uncooperative—the person neither pursues his own concerns nor those of the other individual, thus does not deal with the conflict at all.

Collaborating is a combination of assertive and cooperative behaviours where an individual will attempt to work with others to find a solution that completely satisfies both parties.

Compromising involves a medium degree of both assertiveness and cooperativeness with an intention to find a quick and easy solution that partially satisfies both parties.

In the following story, team members Alan, Christina and Robin are demonstrating recently developed functionality to the Product Owner, Lauren, but they don't get the response they were hoping for and we see how easily conflict can arise. Thankfully, Suranne returns to help the team find a respectful way to proactively use conflict as a source of growth as a team.

Push The Envelope

A good team respects those around them.
A great team challenges their surroundings.

"Whoa!" said Lauren, the team's Product Owner. "You've got that completely the wrong way around. The users will need to capture the information on this screen BEFORE the information on the previous screen. That just doesn't make any sense," she said.

Alan, one of the developers demonstrating this new functionality, was a little lost for words to begin with. He took a couple of seconds to gather his thoughts before responding:

"Well, we took the requirements we were given and asked a few times for people to check things were correct." Alan said, "and the user can definitely get all the information they need to complete the application."

"Yes, technically it works but they won't do it that way. That's not the way it works in the real world Alan," Lauren retorted, loudly.

"If it is that important, why wasn't it specified to begin with?" Alan countered. It was beginning to turn into an argument.

"OK. I see we've got an issue here but perhaps this isn't the time or place to resolve it," Christina, another member of the development team interrupted. "It can't be changed right now and we have a number of other things we need to go through in the next twenty minutes."

"If you think the other features are more important than getting this one right then fine," said Lauren. "I will pick it up with your boss, Henrik, later but it can't go live like this."

After a few tense moments, another developer, Robin, took over the demonstration of the next feature and the review session continued. At the end of the meeting, both Lauren and Alan got up abruptly and left without saying goodbye while Robin, Christina and the rest of the team looked at each other with raised eyebrows.

Before the room had been tidied up, Henrik, the team's line manager, had popped in.

"I've just had Lauren come to see me," Henrik said. "She's not happy. Do you know where Alan is?"

"He left already. He was a bit upset so we just left him to it," Christina replied.

"Not a bad idea," Henrik said, "but I don't think we should leave this too long before we resolve it. I've asked Lauren to come back after lunch for a debrief session to see if we can nip this in the bud. Can you find Alan and all come to see me at 2pm?"

The rest of the team agreed and went to find Alan. He was in the canteen, pacing up and down with an iced latte.

"The bloody nerve!" he almost shouted before Robin made a gesture to suggest he should lower his voice in a public setting.

"I'm sorry," he said, lowering his voice, "but how patronising was she in that meeting?!"

"I tell you what," he continued. "I'm not going to work on anything of hers now unless she has completely specified everything in the minutest level of detail. And I'm going to find the emails that she was copied in on that confirmed this process flow so she can't force us to change it."

"I can see you're still angry, and I can understand where you're coming from, trust me," said Christina, "but we've got to meet her and talk it through professionally after lunch in Henrik's office. And, as frustrating as that might be, it's probably the right thing to do." [Card AC3]

"Oh great!" said Alan, his words dripping with sarcasm.

"Come on. Let's go for a walk outside, you can rant and get things off your chest then we can work out how we are going to handle that meeting," Robin said before the three of them headed outside.

When everyone turned up at Henrik's office, there were polite, if somewhat stiff, greetings before Henrik gave a brief introduction.

"Thanks to everyone for coming at such short notice. I understand there was a difference of opinion in the review session earlier. I don't know the details and don't actually need to know them. I'm just concerned that a professional working relationship doesn't turn sour and my experience says that the longer something like this is left, the more it festers, so it's better to tackle it early."

"I want to introduce you to Suranne," Henrik continued, gesturing towards the lady that was also in the room. "I don't believe any of you know her and that's the point. She has a track record of helping people work through challenging situations and come out with stronger bonds than when they went into the room with her. I'm going to step out now because I can't be truly impartial, but Suranne can."

Suranne introduced herself, explained that she worked in another part of the business and, although moderation or conflict resolution were not in her job description, she has indeed successfully managed to help others resolve differences.

"I can promise both confidentiality and neutrality and my only goal is to help you all find a level of satisfaction with your future working relationship. I think it's only fair for you to know that I operate on the principle that everyone acts with good intentions based on their understanding of the situation," Suranne said. "Based on that, I need to know if you are all happy for me to help you. I cannot and will not impose my help on the situation."

Everyone agreed and Suranne told them all that their first task was to agree a common goal for the session.

"Could you all write down on a separate piece of paper the answer to this question please?" Suranne said before writing the following on the whiteboard at the front of the room:

> **When we find a way to successfully work together, what great thing will we be able to achieve?**

This future-based question assumed success was at least possible and therefore allowed everyone to think positively. Between them they came up with a number of similar statements mostly focused around the success of the new product and all the benefits that would bring.

"That sounds great," Suranne said, "and something definitely worth working for. Now I understand something didn't quite go to plan earlier on. What I would like you to do is think of one thing that happened and write it down in a particular format. The reason I am asking you to do this is to allow you to think carefully about the words you use;

I want you to engage your minds rather than your emotions here if possible."

Suranne then went on to explain the SBI Feedback Model [9] and asked everyone to think of one specific situation, an objective behaviour they observed and the impact that behaviour had on them.

"The most important part of this is for the behaviour to be objective – that is, nobody could debate that it happened. Also, please own the impact, try not to say how you think that behaviour impacted anyone else."

Once everyone had written down their observation, Suranne asked each person in turn to read theirs out, starting alphabetically, with Alan.

"During the review session," Alan began, "Lauren told me that things didn't work that way in the real world but I don't ...."

"Sorry to interrupt you there Alan," said Suranne, "I didn't really explain it properly but the point of this part isn't to debate the behaviours. You did well to name an objective behaviour you observed. Can I ask what impact that statement had on you?"

"I felt patronised, like I didn't live in the real world," said Alan.

"Perfect. Thank you Alan," Suranne responded, before turning to Lauren and saying, "I don't want you to respond to that just yet, Lauren. Instead, I would like you to read out what you observed."

"OK. Well the situation is the same so, during the same review session, I observed a piece of functionality that didn't work the way it was supposed to and I immediately thought of how the hundreds of users would think I hadn't paid attention to their workflow when I went to see them and how I was going to have lost a lot of goodwill with them."

Robin was next and his response was, "During the review session, we discovered something important that we had missed about the functionality, then Lauren and Alan had a disagreement and I felt really uncomfortable presenting the rest of the features."

Robin was pointing out that the misunderstanding between Alan and Lauren was valuable information although both parties seemed to treat it as an embarrassing or useless failure. Great teams are able to learn from so-called "failures" such as this [Card AC4].

Suranne continued to facilitate this conversation and everyone got a greater understanding of why people acted the way they did and the impact this had. There was even a fair degree of self-understanding as empathy was built up across the members of the team.

After everyone had a greater understanding of one another and a greater commitment to collective success, Suranne introduced a conflict model called the Thomas Kilmann Conflict Mode Instrument (TKI).

After briefly explaining the model, Suranne asked each individual to reflect on which mode they adopted during the review session and to consider what each of the alternative modes might have looked like had they adopted them instead.

As a result, they all agreed that there was a lot of *competition* and a lot of *avoiding* with a token attempt at compromising which resulted in a lot of frustration. They discussed what *collaboration* might have looked like and all agreed that this type of behaviour would be the most likely to help them achieve the goal they set out at the beginning of the workshop. Indeed, the passion shown by both Alan and Lauren would be even more useful if they could channel it into a respectful, mutually beneficial argument [Card AC5].

Emotional Intelligence

As well as helping the team and Lauren deal with the specific situation at hand, Suranne was attempting to help the participants increase their levels of Emotional Intelligence (EI). EI is a term that was first popularised by Daniel Goleman [10] and then defined by Salovey and Mayer as *"the ability to monitor one's own and other people's emotions, to discriminate between different emotions and label them appropriately, and to use emotional information to guide thinking and behaviour."* [11]

While there is still debate as to whether EI is actually a valid form of intelligence, there is little doubt in my mind that having a greater understanding of your own emotions and those of others is a significant aid to building better relationships and being more effective in your behaviour.

Once we have greater awareness of our own EI, we can begin to manage our actions more deliberately rather than allow our raw emotions to drive our behaviours. Only then can we hope to influence the situation around ourselves. Understanding the emotions and drivers behind other's actions will then allow us to more positively influence our interactions with other people.

> *What needs to be said but has been avoided for fear of upsetting the team dynamic?*

As a result of the greater EI developed within this facilitated conflict resolution session, the working relationship between Lauren and the rest of the team improved greatly. Of course, changes to the ways of working still needed to be made but they were approached in a much more tactful, respectful and emotionally intelligent manner than before.

The team agreed that having functionality that technically worked but would be unused or worked around by the end users was close to pointless and so wanted to find a way to build the user experience into the team's definition of done. The team agreed that this discussion would make them much more comfortable in the future to "fess up" if and when they make mistakes in the future rather than hide behind the argument of "incomplete requirements" [Card AC6].

Acting purely on emotions, Alan would have insisted that Lauren document this in detail in advance but, by collaborating, they found alternative ways to solve this problem. A new team member was introduced to help mentor the team in the principles of UX while the team were also able to observe the users in action to understand how their functionality would work.

Permission to Challenge

Processes become obsolete very quickly in complex domains and so team-level autonomy is needed for work to be delivered in a rapid yet valuable manner. In order for this to work, great teams need to feel safe to challenge the way things are done and, in some cases, to not even ask for permission [Card AC7].

> *Assuming the people involved have good intentions, why does their current behaviour make perfect sense?*

No matter how strange or frustrating an aspect of organisational policy appears, at some point, somebody thought it was a good idea and that person was unlikely to be doing that for evil purposes. Great teams challenge the status quo [Card AC8], but do so respectfully.

Breaking away from habits or institutionalised practices is difficult and can require huge amounts of creativity [Card AC9] and when faced with something unknown and complex, great teams identify as many options as they can to find a novel way of approaching a situation [Card AC10].

Good teams will respectfully share what needs to happen for them to feel safe and be more proactive. However, great teams will just as ruthlessly look inwards and reflect on how their actions could be making it harder for those around them to trust them with greater autonomy.

SUMMARY

Great teams:

- Challenge the status quo respectfully
- Extract learning from misunderstandings
- Empathise with those they are dealing with
- Admit when they make mistakes
- Assume everyone has good intentions

TRY THIS:

Find a policy or process that is impeding your team. Write down all the possible reasons why this was/is a good thing and prepare a respectful proposal for why it should be changed.

D

S Q U A D

Delivery

"Customers don't measure you on how hard you tried.
They measure you on what you deliver."

Steve Jobs

Delivery

One of the biggest concerns with enabling a team to be autonomous is the concern that, left to their own devices, they simply won't deliver. Many traditional organisations have been built upon the belief that people need to be managed in order to deliver results and, in some cases, that may still be true.

However, in complex domains such as product and/or software development, granting autonomy to cross-functional and self-organising teams is widely considered to be the more effective solution [1].

Even though a well-run self-managing team is more successful and productive than the sum of its individual parts, a team that is new to self-organisation will often see an initial dip in productivity as those team members learn to work well with one another [2]. Therefore, it takes courage and commitment to achieve the benefits of teamwork.

We have seen throughout this book how teams will encounter a number of delivery-related challenges on their journey to mastery.

Firstly, we saw in the *Self-Improvement* section that taking time out to improve the product, our skills, and the processes we are using can also lead to a short-term reduction in delivery.

Great teams are also insistent on building *Quality* into their work but that doesn't come for free either. Then, in the *Unity* section, we saw that self-managing teams also need to get to know one another and find a way to work together as a team towards a clear, compelling and unifying goal.

Finally, the *Audacity* required to challenge the status quo and redefine new ways of working within the team and the wider organisation can also contribute to an apparent slow-down. Integrating all elements of the lifecycle into one short timebox rather than having a sequential, waterfall process [Card DC1] can seem slower from the outside.

But great teams do not let their focus on quality, self-improvement, unity or anything else get in the way of actually delivering results. Indeed, the number one positive factor cited in retrospectives I have facilitated is around the topic of getting work done.

When an organisation switches their focus from *managing for results* to designing environments where teams *can create results,* great teams flourish.

Great teams are in it to deliver. Yes, they want to enjoy their work; yes, they want to be part of a successful team and to take pride in their work. But, in the end, they want to actually produce something that adds value and that they can put their name to and think "I did that".

In our next story, we meet three teams – the Canaries, the Lions and the Gators – who are all trying to deliver value as best they can for Marnus, their Product Owner, but ultimately realise that, sometimes, delivering real value requires a complete shake-up of what we previously considered to be a team.

Self-Manage To Deliver

A good team will do what is required of them to deliver.
A great team will reorganise to optimise delivery.

"It doesn't work that way, Marnus. Usman doesn't get to choose who does their work ... no stakeholder does," Roo, a developer on the Canaries team, stated assertively to Marnus, the Product Owner.

"I hear you, but Usman's got a point. You and the Canaries don't have all the skills necessary to do this within your team," Marnus explained.

"Neither do the Lions, so why is he insisting that they do it?" Roo asked, getting defensive.

"I think he's going on his experience of them working things out for him in the past," Marnus suggested. "They've got a history of somehow managing to get things done against the odds."

The atmosphere was getting a little awkward. Marnus was the Product Owner of three teams and this was a joint planning session of the Canaries, Lions and Gators. All of these teams had a history of reliability when it came to delivering against their forecasts [Card DC2] but it seemed to be getting harder and harder for teams to forecast with confidence, and then get things "done done" by themselves these days [Card DC3].

"I know you are a big fan of teams pulling their own work Roo," said Marnus, "and I know it's not agile for work to be pushed onto teams."

"Yeah. We're supposed to be trusted to figure out how to do what the business needs to be done. After all, we know our skills, capabilities and capacities better than anyone else does," replied Roo.

"And I have seen first-hand how you have all grasped the autonomy offered to you and done great things," Marnus said, attempting to rebuild the relationship before it deteriorated. "It's just that Usman sees the Lions as having a reputation for getting work done, regardless of who has what skills within the team."

"From what I can see, the Lions seem to focus less on each team member trying to be the most productive they could be individually, and more on maximising the overall throughput of work," Marnus offered, as tactfully as he could.

"It's true that they do have more people who are flexible to work on more than one thing if they are needed to," Roo said.

"Is there anything that would help the Canaries become more able to confidently work like this?" asked Marnus.

"Well, I've got my ideas but before I contaminate the airwaves with my opinions, I'm going to see what others think," Roo said, before getting up and grabbing a whiteboard pen. She drew out the following grid.

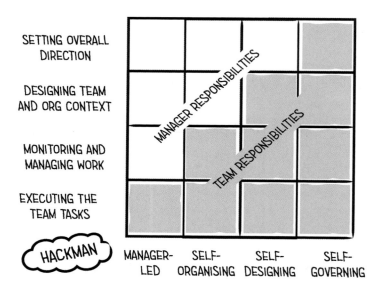

SETTING OVERALL
DIRECTION

DESIGNING TEAM
AND ORG CONTEXT

MONITORING AND
MANAGING WORK

EXECUTING THE
TEAM TASKS

MANAGER RESPONSIBILITIES

TEAM RESPONSIBILITIES

HACKMAN

| MANAGER-LED | SELF-ORGANISING | SELF-DESIGNING | SELF-GOVERNING |

"This is a grid to show that self-management is not binary, that there are different degrees of self-management. It was created by Richard Hackman [3] and shows that the management of a team is a balance between what managers are responsible for and what the team is responsible for. I would be interested to see what level of self-management their team currently has," Roo explained.

She then handed everyone a coloured dot with each colour representing their team. Yellow for the Canaries, Green for the Gators and Red for the Lions.

"Take thirty seconds to think and then place your dot where you think your team currently is," Roo suggested.

The results are shown below with a pretty even spread between self-organising and self-designing:

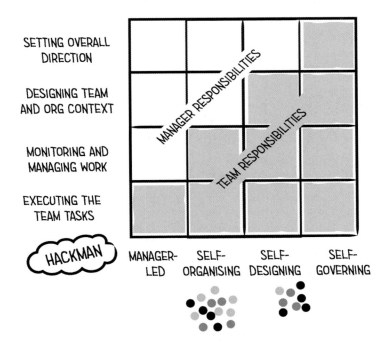

SETTING OVERALL DIRECTION

DESIGNING TEAM AND ORG CONTEXT

MONITORING AND MANAGING WORK

EXECUTING THE TEAM TASKS

MANAGER RESPONSIBILITIES

TEAM RESPONSIBILITIES

HACKMAN

MANAGER-LED   SELF-ORGANISING   SELF-DESIGNING   SELF-GOVERNING

There was a brief discussion about the origins of the team set-up and how the people who had been there longer had felt more involved in the design but were now outnumbered by those who had "inherited" the set-up.

"I wonder if this is an opportunity for us all," said Shannie, from the Gators team.

"An opportunity for what?" asked Roo.

"To think about our team structures. Maybe we need to think about cutting up some dependencies we have across our teams? [Card DC4]. Most of us didn't choose these structures and now we know more about the work, perhaps they could do with a bit of freshening up,"

Shannie explained. "Perhaps we should reorganise ourselves so we can deliver better?" [Card DC5].

"But how?" said Roo.

"How about a Conversation Café? [4]" suggested Shannie.

The teams were familiar with this Liberating Structure [5] and so immediately organised into diverse groups of five or six people. The question that the groups were to consider was:

"Is there a more effective way of organising ourselves to deliver value?"

Shannie quickly wrote up the Conversation Café agreements on the whiteboard at the front of the room as a reminder and handed out a "talking object" to each table from the "props box".

"Thirty minutes and we reconvene."

At the end of the Conversation Café, every group had answered "yes" to the question under discussion but there was no consensus on how they should be organised differently.

"We all seem to think that it is possible to organise ourselves better. Would you be OK with that Marnus?" Shannie asked.

"If it means greater productivity and happier stakeholders then I'm OK with it!" replied Marnus, with a laugh. "But how are we going to decide? And won't it hurt productivity in the short term?"

"Let's try something crazy," suggested Shannie. "I did something like this at my last company and it worked quite well."

Shannie set up an exercise for the three old teams to self-select into three new teams. The only rules were that they needed to do it in complete silence and if they thought there was a better set-up then they should keep moving until they were happy.

There were a number of times when it looked like they had agreed but then people began to move again. Eventually, people became frustrated and asked if they could try something else.

"Can we get someone in to facilitate us?" Roo asked. "Yves is around and I'm sure he wouldn't mind."

Yves was a coach at the company and had worked with the teams on and off in the past. While the team had made a good effort of coaching themselves, great teams realise that they are never so good that some external coaching couldn't be helpful to them. Their willingness to invite Yves in to help them was a sign of humility [Card UC5] that all great teams retain despite their growing confidence.

When Yves came in, he quickly ascertained the main facts of the situation.

Yves confirmed that the teams felt that the current structure – decided by management – wasn't optimal, that the optimal number of teams was three and that the criteria they decided to be important were that they wanted to be able to deliver, add value and grow.

"Based on what you know about us, could you suggest how we could organise ourselves?" asked Roo.

"Sure. But is that the best way to deal with this?" Yves replied. "If you could successfully decide this amongst yourselves, would you prefer that to me deciding for you?"

Most people put their hands up to indicate agreement.

"I think it might just be a case of some missing information that is making this difficult for you. You've been in the same teams for so long now that I'm not sure if you know what everyone else has to offer. Perhaps a Market of Skills and Competency Matrix [6] exercise would give you the information you need to solve this conundrum?" Yves suggested.

"First, I suggest we map out our entire workflow and identify all of the skills and competencies we need to be able to deliver value as teams," said Yves [Card DC6]. Together, they looked back at their definition of done and the product backlog as inspiration before working out the major skills and competencies needed within the team.

Yves then drew up a matrix and asked everyone to rate themselves in terms of their competence level for each of the skills needed to complete the work. They then asked other people to rate them on their skills levels and discussed any wild differences before agreeing an overall competency level. It looked like this:

COMPETENCY	🛠	💭	🧍	📝	📊
ROO	◕	◔	◕	●	◑
SHANNIE	◑	●	◔	◕	◔
SHEILA	◔	◔	◕	○	◑
DEEPAK	○	◕	●	◑	◕
ASHTON	◔	◑	◔	●	◔
NIC	○	◑	◕	◑	◑
MOISES	◕	◔	◑	○	●
CALLUM	◑	○	◕	◑	○
HARRIET	●	◔	◔	◔	○
SURAI	○	◕	◑	◑	◕
CAM	◔	◔	●	◕	◔
ALEX	○	●	◔	◑	●
MACKENZIE	◕	○	○	◕	◑
PRANAV	◑	◔	◕	◔	○
REMY	◔	◑	◑	◕	●
HAZEL	○	◑	◔	◑	◕
KANTU	◔	●	◕	○	◔
CHRIS	●	◔	○	◕	◑

● VERY EXPERIENCED; CAN MENTOR OTHERS   ◔ KNOW THE THEORY BUT LITTLE PRACTICE

◕ SELF-SUFFICIENT   ○ NO KNOWLEDGE OR EXPERIENCE

◑ SOME PRACTICAL EXPERIENCE

He also drew up a template of a Market of Skills [6] poster before encouraging everyone to create their own.

MARKET OF SKILLS

I
SKILLS, KNOWLEDGE AND ABILITIES THAT ARE DIRECTLY RELATED TO THE GOAL OF MY TEAM

II
SKILLS, KNOWLEDGE AND ABILITIES THAT MIGHT – OR MIGHT NOT – BE RELEVANT TO THE GOAL OF MY TEAM

III
WHAT WOULD I LIKE TO LEARN FROM OTHERS IN MY TEAM

By sharing information about skills, experiences and interests, everyone was better equipped to find a better balance and, within twenty minutes, three new teams had been formed. The general consensus was that, although not perfect, they would be an improvement, not just in terms of team chemistry but also their overall ability to deliver more.

> *What skills and competencies are we missing?*
> *What do we have in abundance?*

To Stabilise or Optimise?

Marnus' concern about changing the composition of the current teams is a valid one. Whenever a team changes, even with the intention of improving, there will usually be a blip because that team's rhythm

[Card DC7] has been disrupted. This blip usually follows a J-curve like below:

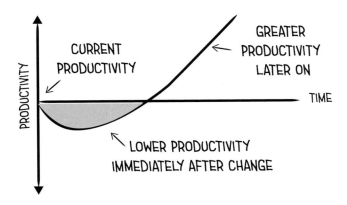

So, there is always an argument for keeping a team stable for a period of time. However, most great teams reach a point where it is in their long-term interests to change things up. Whether that is to freshen the team dynamics with a new face and perspective, or it's to add some new skills or experience or to create room for some more individual growth.

It's never easy to know if or when to change a team's composition – especially if they are doing OK. The old adage of "if it ain't broke, don't fix it" is a hard one to go against but, in this situation, and with most of the great teams I have worked with, it didn't take long to reap the benefits of the new structure.

The teams decided to measure the success of their decision on three factors:

- Are we delivering more and better?
- Are we learning more as individuals and teams?
- Are our stakeholders more satisfied?

Within four weeks, all of these metrics were trending up and the team had already begun the move towards self-government. Not only had they figured out how to design the teams for optimal overall delivery but, because of this higher-level focus, they were also able and keen to input into the overall strategic direction of the teams.

The Pull of Autonomy

Agile teams are intended to be self-managing and autonomous. When operating in complex domains, the people doing the work are generally considered to be the best placed to make decisions about what to do and when to do it. This, coupled with autonomy being a pillar of motivation in more complex domains, means that, for best results, conditions should be created for work to be "pulled" by autonomous teams.

Autonomy is so important to people that you might even find them resisting ideas that are in their own interests simply because they feel they have had the idea imposed upon them and their autonomy compromised.

Team autonomy does not mean the team has completely free rein. The degree of self-organisation will usually be negotiated with management and leadership within the organisation, and not only will different self-organising teams have varying levels of autonomy, but this may change as a team develops and grows over time.

In general, the great teams that I have seen have negotiated a greater level of autonomy in part by cutting away important dependencies in order to have greater control over the whole value-delivery process.

This can be scary for management and leadership but, essentially, when I speak to managers one-on-one and ask them whether they would prefer a team that could successfully look after itself and deliver or one that required greater supervision, I find that it is not the concept that worries them but their scepticism about whether it will work. If they can assume success is inevitable then they regularly choose the self-managed option.

> ### *What benefits would greater team autonomy give the organisation?*

Many groups of people are able to successfully cooperate, but it takes a lot more courage and maturity to collaborate. To cooperate, I simply need to negotiate or compromise with someone. For example, "If you do this for me, then I will do that for you." However, collaboration requires letting go of one's individual agenda and ideas so that the team can build on them with the output being unrecognisable as coming from any individual member of the team.

So why not just cooperate? In many cases this is enough; and many teams can achieve good results through cooperation. But, in my experience, the greater creativity, commitment and energy that comes from successful collaboration is one of the hallmarks of great teams.

In the most extreme of examples, every member of the team may become individually less efficient and productive but the team, as a whole, may deliver more value. And the members of the team will be happy with this. The trade-off of individual efficiency for greater overall effectiveness can seem strange but when there is complexity, innovation and change then being able to pitch in together is much more valuable.

Accountability

Teams that collaborate hold themselves accountable as a team rather than focusing on whether, as an individual, they have delivered "their individual piece" or "done their bit". It's subtly different but creates a fundamentally different dynamic that sets the great teams apart from the good ones. Individuals may be highly productive but if they are not contributing to the team dynamic they may still find their position on the team in question.

Equally, most teams will have someone who may not be the most productive individual but is seen as crucial to overall team harmony and success. Many sports teams have so-called "unsung heroes" who don't attract the spotlight but their unnoticeable presence allows for greater team success. One of the most famous is Horace Grant of the NBA Championship winning 1992 Chicago Bulls. Despite not being the best in any of the individual stats such as point scoring, rebounds, assists etc, the team generally lost when he wasn't playing. Agile teams are no different and organisations are waking up to the fact that a great team requires many types of contribution to be successful.

This obviously poses a problem if our structures and processes are set up to encourage individual productivity and some individuals may be anxious about losing their recognition (and possibly even bonuses) by taking a more team-based approach to work. How do we know who contributed what to the team effort? In a truly great team, this is both impossible to say and unnecessary to ask.

> *What behaviours tend to be under-appreciated and over-appreciated?*

Organisational leaders, product owners and customers don't care about the minutiae of individual contributions; they do care about the overall delivery, and great teams focus on the higher objectives.

In the great teams that I have seen, members place being part of the team, working towards a shared goal, as significantly more important to them than their pay or bonus levels, but be prepared to lose a few people who don't want to be part of a team ethic.

SUMMARY

Great teams:

- Go outside of job descriptions in order to deliver value
- Collaborate rather than just cooperate
- Explicitly negotiate their level of autonomy
- Understand and increase the spread of skills
- Balance stability with growth

TRY THIS:

Run a competency mapping exercise in your team and discuss how you would like to develop greater balance and resilience within the team.

It can take months, if not longer, for some teams to get to a point where they are getting stuff done and delivering actual releasable increments of value to their customers on a regular basis.

A rhythm of delivery [Card DC7] is a very powerful factor behind successful teams; they create their own cadence of work and delivery that they, and others outside of the team, can depend upon. Rhythm and rituals are a great way of combating the inevitable anxiety that comes with the ambiguity and uncertainty of working in a complex domain, so all great teams strive for a predictable pace in their delivery.

The really great teams, however, don't just get into rhythm but also get into what we call *flow* [Card DC8]. You might be more accustomed to the phrase "in the zone" but the term "being in a flow state" is becoming increasingly part of the lexicon of the business world since it was publicised by Mihály Csíkszentmihályi in 1975. [7]

A flow state is defined as "the mental state of operation in which a person performing an activity is fully immersed in a feeling of energised focus, full involvement, and enjoyment in the process of the activity. In essence, flow is characterised by complete absorption in what one does, and a resulting loss in one's sense of space and time." [8]

Don't worry, it's not true that you need to be a great team to be in a flow state. It is rather the case that great teams tend to get into that state more often and learn how to set themselves up to more often achieve it.

When I think of the word "flow" I naturally think of a river and it is a metaphor that fits quite nicely. Rivers can be gentle but can also contain rapids; teams can also trundle along gently with the odd period of apparent turmoil or rapid action. Rivers can be deceptively fast with undercurrents and teams can operate at multiple levels with depth.

Great teams find their pace and rarely follow a straight line to delivery; just like a river and a great way of thinking about the concept of "flow" is when one is swimming with the current. It's amazing how far you can travel and how effortless it can feel.

The following story tells of a team that stumbled across the state of flow and then ritualised their processes to achieve it more often. We join The Full English team in their retrospective and team members Hallie, Declan and Mark are trying something a little different.

Flow Like A River

A good team gets into a rhythm of delivery.
A great team gets into flow.

Hallie drew a random card from the deck and read it out loud to determine the focus for the retrospective.

"If you were to be really brave this sprint, what would you like to try as a team?"

There was a general murmuring of contemplation within the rest of the team.

"What does brave mean in our context?" asked Declan.

"I suppose we could make the assumption that we have been playing it safe the last few sprints, and this is an opportunity to push ourselves outside of our comfort zone; to try something new," Mark suggested.

"I'm not sure I would describe three sprints of delivering on our forecasts as safe," Declan responded, "and I don't think jeopardising that record is a good idea. We've got people on our side; they are happy with our consistency."

"That's true," agreed Hallie, "but maybe we have got more potential that we haven't tapped into yet, and maybe we need to take a risk to see if we can get there."

"The business know that they can rely on us to deliver about ten integrations every month now. Are you talking about increasing that to, say, fifteen?" asked Declan. "You know how we got to this point, right? By slowing down, not by speeding up." His concern was visible.

And Declan was right. The team had indeed needed to slow down and take on less work to get to a point where they could deliver predictably. Since then, their output had been growing slowly as they had mapped out their workflow and incrementally discovered ways to tweak their working practices to become more effective as a team [Card DC6].

"I'm not sure bravery is just about increasing our output. Maybe there are other ways to interpret it. Let's brainstorm it. How about we all just take a couple of minutes to think what the word brave could mean in our context?" Mark suggested.

The rest of the team agreed and set off with sticky notes and marker pens in hand. Ten minutes later, they began collecting their thoughts together. The sticky notes on the wall contained a number of different perspectives, including:

"Cross-skilling within the team to reduce single points of excellence."
"Trying out some new technologies."
"Expanding the engineering practices."
"Expanding the technical aspect of the definition of done."

As each sticky note was read out and stuck to the wall, the rest of the team nodded in agreement with a moderate amount of enthusiasm. Until Hallie stepped up and said:

"Bit crazy I know, but bear with me; I thought maybe we could build an API that would allow us to integrate with our competitors' products."

This time there was no murmuring, no nodding of agreement and Hallie looked a little nervous. She went on to explain, "So far, we have avoided it because it would make it easier for our customers to work with and buy our competitors' products and services. But it could work the other way. What if our competitors' customers are not coming to us because it's too difficult for them?"

"Well, that would certainly qualify as *brave* in my book," said Declan, "bordering on insane!"

"It could work. I don't think technically it would be too difficult but obviously it would have to be a business decision. We would have to pitch it to Fitz," Mark added, appearing to like the idea more the longer he thought about it.

Fitz, the Product Owner, was known to be ambitious and bold, so it took a little time for the team to take to him and also for them to earn his trust. This recent bout of predictability where the team could confidently meet their forecasts [Card DC1] had improved their relationship fantastically. Fitz loved having the confidence to be able to say to stakeholders and customers when they could expect their integrations to be delivered.

"Personally, I would be a bit nervous about mentioning the idea to Fitz before we knew whether it would actually work. I wouldn't want to get his hopes or his interest up and then let him down," said Hallie.

"So how about we see if we can do a proof of concept this sprint and present it to him at the sprint review?" Mark asked.

The next sprint had a different energy about it and it was mentioned a few times during their daily meetings. Hallie once described it as feeling as though they were being "a little bit naughty, but in a good way".

This energy was infectious and, on more than one occasion, the team members commented that they felt like they were "in the zone" and that the days often seemed to fly by. The term "flow" was mentioned more than once and before they knew it the team were playing around with the proof of concept in their own time and even buying licences for third-party software out of their own pockets.

Just before the sprint review, they called Fitz for a pre-meeting chat and showed him what they had come up with.

"I LOVE IT!" he exclaimed. "I mean, sure it's a little bit risky but the sales team could go crazy with this. Can we use this to pitch directly to clients?" he asked.

"With a little bit of tweaking, we could get it to *done done*, yes," Hallie replied [Card DC3].

"Then let me demonstrate it in the sprint review. We're going to blow their minds with this one!" Fitz said.

During the sprint review, Fitz used his charisma and energy to convince everyone that this was a game changer and he wanted to dedicate the whole of the next sprint to bringing this to life. The stakeholders agreed and the team couldn't wait to get back to turning the proof of concept into reality.

During the next sprint, they paired up promiscuously [9], even mob programming [10] at times and they felt like they had achieved much more than they ever had in a sprint before [Card DC4]. Being brave had opened up a whole new strategic direction for the company.

Get Rhythm

The team in the story above had already achieved the primary aim of most agile teams; they established a predictable cadence of delivery. This is a huge benefit to an organisation for many reasons.

Firstly, knowing that a team *can* deliver regularly makes it easier to manage expectations of stakeholders. Even if the news is undesirable – we won't have your work done within six weeks – it is a lot easier to take if it is reliable news. People are much more upset and unreasonable when they are told it will take six weeks and then for it to end up taking longer.

Secondly, everyone in an agile environment is operating in a context of uncertainty, ambiguity and volatility. In general, these factors increase levels of anxiety in people as we crave certainty and predictability. So, given that change and uncertainty is non-negotiable, having a rhythm and cadence that we can work to and rely on makes people much more comfortable. And when we are comfortable, we can do better work and make better decisions.

> *How predictable is your pace of delivery right now?*

Get Flow

Once we have rhythm and we have a sense of confidence and safety in our working practices, we open ourselves up to the possibility of getting into flow [Card DC8]. Flow is very difficult to define but it's one of those states that "you know it when you see it".

Often, we only actually notice it when we come out of it. This is because when we are in flow, everything else seems to melt away and we become so absorbed in what we do that we don't notice anything else going on around us.

As in the story above, energy levels are high and stress levels are low, creativity is high and awareness of time is low. It is an incredibly motivating, fulfilling and productive state that, once a team has experienced, they want to return to. It is like a drug.

Flow is notoriously hard to consciously create; almost as difficult as trying to recall your dream upon waking in the morning. There are some things that great teams have consistently cited as helping increase the chances of getting into flow though. Put simply, it is finding a balance between challenge and boredom.

"High challenge leads to anxiety and low challenge to boredom. Right in the middle is the area where flow is possible."

- Daniel Levitin [11]

If there is too much pressure – perhaps from a lack of preparation or practise for the task at hand – then performance drops to a minimum as the team feel overloaded and it eventually leads to burnout. On the other hand, a lack of purpose or challenge will lead to boredom and eventually rustout.

Prepare – Continually develop your skills. If we don't feel capable of the tasks at hand, we will not achieve flow. Instead we will create anxiety. A little bit of mindfulness can also be great preparation.

Practise – Get to a point where some of what you do becomes almost automatic. Think about your commute to work and how often you go on "auto pilot" and don't remember getting there. You were in flow.

Purpose – Make sure there is a compelling and challenging reason for you and the team to put the effort in. Find out who will benefit and why that is important [Card DC9]. It has to be difficult enough to feel like a challenge, but not so difficult that it seems impossible.

These three "Ps" are represented by the Burnout-Rustout graph below.

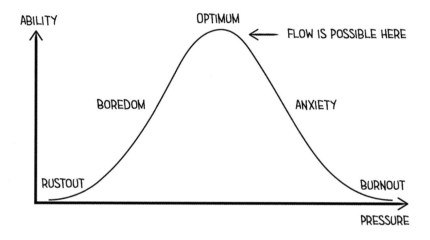

There are three more Ps to help us increase the chances of getting into flow and they are:

Protection – Create a container where you can work as a team without being distracted for a while.

Parity – Try and create an environment where every member of the team feels on the same "level" as one another and has the safety to act.

Pomodoro – The Pomodoro technique is a simple exercise for timeboxing and focus. Simply set a timer for twenty-five minutes and focus on that, and nothing else, for that long. Then break. [12]

> *How could you create a safer container that could*
> *increase the chances of getting into flow?*

Teams cannot stay in a state of flow forever; it is the exception to one's working week rather than the norm. Although, according to Levitin, flow is still largely elusive, "involving a particular neurochemical soup that has not yet been identified", teams can increase their time in a state of flow and the number of times they enter flow through conscious practise and reflection.

Levitin argues that "almost without exception, the flow state is when one does his or her best work, in fact, work that is above and beyond what one normally thinks of as his or her best." Indeed, I have seen how the amazing results of a team being in a state of flow can catch the attention of people within the organisation and, without careful understanding, lead to unrealistic expectations for future performance.

This was the case with the team in the story above. After such a game-changing innovation from the team, the sales team did indeed "go crazy" as Fitz predicted. This led to an increase in demand and more budget was made available to expand the team with new hires.

> *A good team knows when to speed up.*
> *A great team knows when to slow down.*

"Let's double the team straight away. We've got so many new customers that we can afford to hire a whole new team and then we can double the amount of integrations we can deliver," said Fitz, with his usual bullish enthusiasm.

"I can see you are excited Fitz, and we are too, but I don't think it works quite as easily as that," said Mark, nervous about coming across as the party pooper. "I really think we need to grow slowly. I think we should set aside one whole month to on-board the new people. I genuinely believe that slowing down is our best chance of being able to speed up."

"A month?! And we would have no integrations or deliveries in that timeframe? That's a big ask Mark."

"I know," replied Mark. "But they have a lot to learn and we don't want to undo what we've worked so hard to create. If it works, then they will be more likely to hit the ground running."

"Our suggestion is to create some practical assignments for them so that they can learn the ropes on the actual systems, then we will ask them to teach back what they have learned about what we have built from the perspective of the user," added Hallie.

"This way, we will get an independent, fresh insight into what we have done and they will learn first-hand rather than be taught from our biased perception," said Declan.

"OK. I think I can keep the stakeholders at bay for one month, but it won't be easy. I'm only doing this because of the goodwill you created with Trojan." [Trojan was the nickname for the competitor integration the team built during their "brave" sprint.]

After the onboarding process, the team decided to stay as one large team rather than split into two smaller teams and things went well to start with, mainly because of the onboarding time invested.

Eventually though, the extra communication required to keep everyone in the team up to speed with what was happening began to deteriorate; fewer people were talking to each other; moments of flow were fewer and further between and so the decision was made to split into two teams.

Mark called Fitz to one side after a relatively listless sprint review. "You're not going to like this Fitz, but we really think we need to slow down again so that we can make this split work properly. We need to figure out how we should organise the two teams so there is a good balance of experience, skills, personality and the like.

"The good news," he added, "is that we won't need a month this time. Our plan is to try a new set-up next sprint and then inspect and adapt it at the end of the sprint. We will just work on less to give us time to work on the team dynamics at the same time."

Fitz reluctantly agreed, swayed by the argument that there would be a higher chance of getting back to the energy and creativity levels of the past if the teams were smaller. After Fitz had agreed in principle to the team's request, Mark took what he felt was another audacious step.

"How would you feel about coming along to the retrospective to help us figure out how to do that?" Mark asked. "We've been thinking it would be great to get you involved in those meetings for a while, if you're up for it."

"Of course I'd be up for it," Fitz replied. "You were worried about asking me?"

"Well it was kind of the team's safe space where we could figure things out and come up with something more sensible before wasting your time or risking judgement," Mark said, a little embarrassed.

"Any improvements you make are only going to benefit me and the sooner I know what you are thinking, the earlier I can help," explained Fitz.

"Yeah, and we were just plucking up the courage as a team to invite you. Now I wish we had done that sooner."

The changes that the team made, including involving Fitz in the retrospective, had a great impact. Within four weeks, the two smaller teams were delivering much more than the one bigger team ever delivered; and the instances of flow began increasing again [Card DC10].

Like most rivers, a team will spend most of its time gently meandering and flowing slowly but steadily. Every now and again the conditions are just right for some temporary excitement and a significant increase in pace. Our team here were spurred on by the safety they had created through their predictable level of delivery and the challenge of being braver.

They had the support and the container to try something different, something energising and something that felt "a little bit naughty" as Hallie put it. Getting into flow certainly has a different feel to it, and a different energy, and can become a little addictive, just as white water rafting can be addictive for river-runners.

A river does not continue increasing its pace indefinitely though and great teams do not either. Indeed, flow does not always involve speeding up. Somewhat counter-intuitively, flow can involve slowing down in order to speed up. Getting things together, building up energy, and gathering a focus is something that great teams are not afraid of. This conscious management of rhythm and flow is a hallmark of all great teams.

SUMMARY

Great teams:

- Establish a predictable rhythm of delivery
- Work to get into a flow state regularly
- Are prepared to slow down in order to speed up
- Create a safe space where everyone can contribute
- Find the sweet spot between burnout and rustout

TRY THIS:

Think back to a time when you were last in a state of flow. Replicate as many of the conditions that contributed to that and see if it works again. Keep trying.

Conclusion

Many years ago, I was feeling a little down and, after I had explained my thoughts, my coach at the time asked me whether I was someone who enjoyed the journey or the destination. I was intrigued by this and reflected on it a lot. I realised that I was very "achievement driven" and worked from one achievement to another as quickly as possible. I wasn't looking at the scenery along the way or enjoying being a "work in progress" and so, when something took a long time, I tended to get frustrated.

I tell you this because we have now seen many of the hallmarks of Team Mastery and how much time, energy and courage are needed to become a great team. It is a never-ending journey because, even if you arrive at the ultimate destination and become the best team in the world, that will only be temporary unless you continue to grow and develop.

Even though it is inevitably a tough and unending commitment, it is one that every great team I know considers worthwhile. Being part of a great team is not only a prerequisite to achieve great things these days, but is also hugely fulfilling.

Once you have decided to work towards becoming a great team, you will forge your own path; you cannot copy what worked for another team. Your team is unique and growth is a continual journey with many twists and turns and plenty of ups and downs. There will be times when you wonder if it's worth it and times when you seem to be going backwards, but those are often the times where you grow the most.

My hope is that this book will help you enjoy the journey and celebrate the interim successes with the milestone cards I have included and then create your own as you hit your own unique milestones. Embrace the fact that you are perfectly imperfect and always improving and growing towards Team Mastery – you can do it, and it's worth it!

References

Introduction

[1] Tuckman, B.W. (1965) "Developmental sequence in small groups."
Psychological Bulletin. 63 (6): 384–399. https://psycnet.apa.org/doiLanding?doi=10.1
037%2Fh0022100. PMID 14314073.

[2] Lencioni, P.M. (2010) Overcoming the Five Dysfunctions of a Team. Hoboken,
N.J.: Jossey-Bass.

Self-Improvement

[1] https://agilemanifesto.org/principles.html

[2] Dweck, C.S. (2006) Mindset: The new psychology of success. Random House.

[3] Duckworth, A. (2013) Grit: The power of passion and perseverance.
https://www.ted.com/talks/
angela_lee_duckworth_grit_the_power_of_passion_and_perseverance

[4] Goldratt, E.M., 1947-2011. (2004) The goal: a process of ongoing improvement.
Great Barrington, MA: North River Press.

[5] https://www.tastycupcakes.org/2013/05/the-penny-game/

[6] Martin, K. & Osterling, M. (2013) Value Stream Mapping: How to Visualise Work.

[7] https://en.wikipedia.org/wiki/Causal_loop_diagram

[8] https://www.agilealliance.org/glossary/three-amigos/

[9] Pink, D. (2009) The Puzzle of Motivation.
https://www.ted.com/talks/dan_pink_on_motivation

[10] Edmondon, A. (2014) Building a Psychologically Safe Workplace. youtube.com/watch?v=LhoLuui9gX8

[11] https://jamesclear.com/marginal-gains

[12] https://www.willitmaketheboatgofaster.com/

[13] https://www.tinyhabits.com/

[14] https://www.hsdinstitute.org/resources/cde-model.html

[15] https://en.wikipedia.org/wiki/Asch_conformity_experiments

[16] http://cognitive-edge.com/blog/abide-overview-of-process/

Quality

[1] https://www.mountaingoatsoftware.com/blog/defect-management-by-policy-a-fast-easy-approach-to-prioritizing-bug-fixes

[2] Martin, R., Feathers, M., Ottinger, T., Langr, J., Schuchert, B., Grenning, J., Wampler, K. & Coplien, J. (2011) Clean code. Upper Saddle River [etc.]: Prentice Hall.

[3] https://pragprog.com/magazines/2010-06/the-mikado-method

[4] https://en.wikipedia.org/wiki/Technical_debt#Service_or_repay_the_technical_debt

[5] Loss aversion. (2019, October 16) Retrieved October 29, 2019, from https://en.wikipedia.org/wiki/Loss_aversion

[6] Sheetz, M. (2017, August 24) Technology killing off corporate America: Average life span of companies under 20 years. Retrieved October 29, 2019, from https://www.cnbc.com/2017/08/24/technology-killing-off-corporations-average-lifespan-of-company-under-20-years.html

[7] Ferriss, T. (2018, August 22) Fear-Setting: The Most Valuable Exercise I Do Every Month. Retrieved October 29, 2019, from https://tim.blog/2017/05/15/fear-setting/

[8] https://en.wikipedia.org/wiki/Cynefin_framework

[9] http://cognitive-edge.com/videos/cynefin-framework-introduction/

[10] https://www.urbandictionary.com/define.php?term=bouncebackability

[11] Kahn, W. A. (1990-12-01) "Psychological Conditions of Personal Engagement and Disengagement at Work". Academy of Management Journal. 33 (4): 692–724.

[12] Harford, T. (n.d.). Trial, error and the God complex. Retrieved from https://www.ted.com/talks/tim_harford

[13] Duke, A. (2018) Thinking in bets: making smarter decisions when you don't have all the facts. New York: Portfolio/Penguin.

Unity

[1] Csíkszentmihályi, M. (2016) Flow and the Foundations of Positive Psychology: the Collected Works of Mihály Csíkszentmihályi. Dordrecht: Springer.

[2] Yong, E. (2009) Rowing as a group increases pain thresholds. National Geographic. https://www.nationalgeographic.com/science/phenomena/2009/09/15/rowing-as-a-group-increases-pain-thresholds/ Published September 15, 2009. Accessed October 29, 2019.

[3] https://www.tonyrobbins.com/mind-meaning/do-you-need-to-feel-significant/

[4] https://www.hgi.org.uk/human-givens/introduction/what-are-human-givens

[5] https://en.wikipedia.org/wiki/Maslow's_hierarchy_of_needs

[6] Turner, J.C. & Reynolds, K.J. (2010) "The story of social identity". In Postmes, T. & Branscombe, N. (eds.). Rediscovering Social Identity: Core Sources. Psychology Press.

[7] Goddard, P. (2015) Improv-Ing Agile Teams: Using Constraints to Unlock Creativity. Bradford: Agilify Ltd.

[8] Tuckman, B.W. (1965) Developmental sequence in small groups. Psychological Bulletin. 63(6):384-399. doi:10.1037/h0022100.

[9] Katzenbach, J.R. & Smith, D.K. (2015) The Wisdom of Teams: Creating the High-Performance Organization. Boston, MA: Harvard Business Review Press.

[10] https://www.pminj.org/14-smp/files/ckirby-ho.pdf

[11] https://liveingreatness.com/core-protocols/

[12] https://qz.com/1046131/writing-a-user-manual-at-work-makes-teams-less-anxious-and-more-productive/

[13] https://www.thefreedictionary.com/bantering

[14] https://www.youtube.com/watch?v=6C9NxPkyVsU&gl=GB

[15] https://en.wikipedia.org/wiki/Ishin-denshin

Audacity

[1] https://edition.cnn.com/2015/10/29/health/science-of-fear/index.html

[2] https://en.wikipedia.org/wiki/Endowment_effect

[3] Landsberg, M., (2003) The Tao of Coaching: Boost Your Effectiveness at Work by Inspiring and Developing Those Around You, Profile Books.

[4] https://liveingreatness.com/core-protocols/perfection-game/

[5] https://www.ccl.org/articles/leading-effectively-articles/closing-the-gap-between-intent-and-impact/

[6] http://www.if-dev.co.uk/wp-content/uploads/2013/07/BEEF-Feedback.pdf

[7] https://management30.com/practice/kudo-cards/

[8] https://kilmanndiagnostics.com/overview-thomas-kilmann-conflict-mode-instrument-tki/

[9] Use the SBI Feedback Model to Understand Intent: CCL. https://www.ccl.org/articles/leading-effectively-articles/closing-the-gap-between-intent-and-impact/ Published April 14, 2019. Accessed October 30, 2019.

[10] http://www.danielgoleman.info/topics/emotional-intelligence/

[11] https://psycnet.apa.org/doiLanding?doi=10.1037/1528-3542.1.3.232

Delivery

[1] Pink, D. (2009) The Puzzle of Motivation. https://www.ted.com/talks/dan_pink_the_puzzle_of_motivation

[2] Katzenbach, J. R. & Smith, D. K. (1993) The Wisdom of Teams, Harvard Business School Press

[3] Hackman, J.R. (2002) Leading Teams. Harvard Business School Press.

[4] http://www.liberatingstructures.com/17-conversation-cafe/

[5] http://www.liberatingstructures.com/ls-menu/

[6] https://blog.crisp.se/2012/11/06/anderslaestadius/team-liftoff-with-market-of-skills-and-competence-matrix

[7] Csíkszentmihályi, M. (2016) Flow and the Foundations of Positive Psychology: the Collected Works of Mihály Csíkszentmihályi. Dordrecht: Springer.

[8] https://en.wikipedia.org/wiki/Flow_(psychology)

[9] https://csis.pace.edu/~grossman/dcs/XR4-PromiscuousPairing.pdf

[10] https://www.agilealliance.org/glossary/mob-programming/

[11] Levitin, D.J. (2015) The Organised Mind: Thinking Straight in the Age of Information Overload. London: Viking.

[12] https://en.wikipedia.org/wiki/Pomodoro_Technique

Credits

This book was given the chance of creation because a number of people showed faith in me and my idea by paying money upfront via a Kickstarter campaign. I really appreciate every one of them and some even paid extra to have their name appear in the credits. Below is where we will record their generosity:

Alex Jeffrey	Christoph Möbius	Katy Chandler-Grant
Alistair Williams	Claire Brown	Liviu Mesesan
Allan McPike	Dan Kastelik	M N Parkes
Andreas G. Wittler	David Reid	Rolf Irion
Arun Chinnaraju	Erin Quick-Laughlin	Samuel Lau
Ash Ganatra	Gareth Cooney	Simon Reindl
Ash Tiwari	Gareth Thomas	Stephen Smith
Barry Overeem	Ian Hutchison	Steven Crossland
Björn Jensen	Ines Garcia	Tony Marsh
Carsten Grønbjerg Lützen	John Leighton	Vikki Price
Christine Murray	Jon McNestrie	Yolanda V. Martinez

And thank you to Scott Logic who promised to buy a bulk batch of books.

During the process of writing this book, I took what felt like a big risk and opened myself and my writing process up to strangers right from the start. It was scary for people to be able to see the book (and sometimes me!) at its worst, but it was incredibly valuable.

The following people not only helped support the Kickstarter campaign but also were some of the first to take the leap. These people not only offered financial backing but also shared their time, experience and knowledge to collaborate with me during the process:

Aislinn Holmes	Georg Fasching	Mark Kilby
Arnold H. Panganiban	Graz Kania-Knight	Robb Lockwood
Benjamin Sommer	Greg Pitcher	Robin Hackshall
Chris McLaughlin	Jamie Collins	Ruth Guthoff-Recknagel
Claire Donald	Jon Gedge	Sean Moir
David Klang	Leonidas Vomvoridis	Tony Richards
David Millward	Leslie James Dawes	Wolfgang Döbber
Eva Gysling	Lindsey Sauerlander CSP-SM	Yves Hanoulle

After enjoying working with him so much on my previous books, I once again turned to Ole Størksen. This time I challenged him even further with some demanding illustrations, which he has amazed me with. I also had illustrative help from Frode Karlsen and editorial help from Kelly Owen at Ultimate Proof Ltd.

I am very grateful for Lee Humphries who helped me with the accuracy of the ATLS scenario in the Fail To Succeed story. My good friend, Paul Goddard, helped out once again and I am grateful to him as well as Lyssa Adkins, Ron Jeffries, Andrea Tomasini and Roman Pichler for their helpful interventions, contributions and advice.

I also want to say a special thank you to Tamsen Mitchell who couldn't quite be as involved with this project as much as either she or I wished for.

And of course I couldn't have done this without the support of my family. My wife Alison, my daughter Freya, my son Cody and of course, the inspiration for the milestone cards, my son Grayson

MILESTONE CARDS

The following cards are pictorial representations of the milestones that I have seen many great teams reach along their journey to Team Mastery. This is not an exhaustive or linear list. Many teams will reach other milestones and some may never reach some of these milestones.

They are structured in the chronological order that I referenced them in the stories earlier in the book.

If your team are looking to develop their self-improvement characteristic then these milestones could be a good source of information and inspiration. Check out the benefits, and the risks, with aiming for this milestone as well as some rituals that you can put in place to increase your chances of success.

Also, if you are looking for more resources to support you then scan the QR code and you will be taken to an ever-evolving page of supporting articles, videos and exercises that can further explain and strengthen your efforts in this area.

If you hit a milestone that isn't captured in one of these cards then use one of the blank cards to illustrate your success and then share that with the rest of the community using the #TeamMastery hashtag.

Great Teams Have SQUAD Depth

Cross-functional, self-organising teams are the beating heart of complex work. While every team is different, with their own unique talents and strengths, I have found that there are a number of common patterns that all of the great teams that I have seen share.

Self-Improvement
Great teams never settle for where they are; they constantly strive to improve. They push the boundaries of what is good and end up creating a new "best".

Quality
Good enough is not good enough for great teams. They take pride in doing things to a high level of quality. They are proud of their work and are happy to be associated with what they create.

Unity
The three musketeers famously said, "One for all and all for one" and this is a common thread in great teams. They consider their team-mates almost as selected family; they have each other's backs and always support one another.

Audacity
Great teams step outside of their comfort zone and dare to be bold. They push boundaries, they are vulnerable, they take personal risks and stand up for integrity.

Delivery
Great teams never forget that they are there to deliver. They are only satisfied when they manage to produce something that is of value to their customers and their users.

Today we took

ACTION

RISKS

The main risks with putting retrospective actions into place are to do with how well the team thinks things through. Do they consider options for how to solve the problem or just latch on to the first idea they come up with? Do they consider how their idea might impact other people, teams or systems? The other main risk is that the team focuses so much on improving things that they forget that they need to continue delivering value, so a healthy balance should be struck.

REWARDS

Too many teams see the same problems come up time after time because they don't resolve an impediment when they find it. This is usually down to being busy, or lacking ownership, but when a team feels the accomplishment of changing their working practices and environment for the better, the energy and morale boost is huge. Their appetite for further improvement and change increases and it becomes infectious. Other teams take notice and begin to believe that they, too, can enhance their own situation.

RITUALS

Take one area for improvement at a time and focus on getting something positive done about it rather than trying to take on too many actions. Identify the value to you as a team of doing something about it. If you can't explain why it is important to you then you will likely not do anything about it. Break it down into something you can progress in the next couple of days and then increase your sense of accountability by telling other people you are going to do it.

RESOURCES

Today we demonstrated a
GROWTH MINDSET

RISKS

Teams can get carried away with an experimental approach when beginning to adopt a growth mindset. They can start off too many experiments rather than focus on improving a small number of things at one time. Admitting that we cannot do something yet takes courage and accepting responsibility for closing that gap. It is often easier to say, "I'm just not blessed with that talent" and not try. If one believes in the concept of a growth mindset and subsequently struggles to develop that skill, then it is easy to judge oneself as failing to achieve something that has just been defined as achievable.

REWARDS

Apart from the immediate benefit of developing a new skill, a growth mindset creates a profound sense of possibility and optimism; an energy that feeds others around you. The belief that anything is possible is powerful and every time that a team collects evidence of this effect it strengthens that belief. Great teams move on from developing their individual and collective talents to challenging previously taboo topics such as structures, processes and policies, eventually proactively shaping the organisation that they are a part of.

RITUALS

To begin with, reduce the pressure by crafting experiments rather than commitments. Test the assumptions around the impossible to see just how impossible things really are. Embrace your "beginner's mind" and remember how daunting the prospect of learning to walk or ride a bicycle was when you were younger. Remind yourself of skills you have already learned throughout your life and commit to enjoy the journey of learning.

RESOURCES

Today we showed

GRIT

RISKS

Grit is defined as "the tendency to sustain perseverance and passion for challenging long-term goals" and, in short, as "stick-ability". Not giving up at your first, second or third attempt is admirable, if indeed your approach has the potential to succeed eventually. If, however, you are on to an inevitable losing battle then you are simply wasting time and resources. By taking the view that all things can be achieved eventually, we risk sending the message that you simply haven't tried hard enough to people who aren't successful.

REWARDS

The feeling of achievement when finally tackling something that was proving difficult is immense and, arguably, nothing of worth was ever achieved without a struggle, so grit is a laudable characteristic to develop individually and within a team. Many aspects of team development as well as valuable work will involve slogging through some tough, perhaps menial and repetitive, aspects and grit will serve us well in these areas. For teams that are developing their independence, grit is an important characteristic to help them through the inevitable growing pains.

RITUALS

To ensure we are not simply banging our heads against the metaphorical wall, we should always and regularly ask whether we believe something is truly possible. Asking "What are we learning?" can help a team turn even the worst situations into growth opportunities. Grit doesn't necessarily involve trying the same approach until it works, experimenting with different methods (perhaps in parallel) can be a valuable habit to adopt too.

RESOURCES

Today we resolved an
IMPEDIMENT

RISKS

There is a risk that a team will optimise at the local level and not at the systems level – simply because of what is visible to them. This resolving of an impediment for them could create an impediment elsewhere. If this needs to be rolled back then the demotivation can be great. There is also a risk that while figuring out where their autonomy ends when it comes to fixing things, they overstep the mark, which can, at best, create unrest personally and organisationally but, at worst, cause serious repercussions.

REWARDS

Teams that proactively resolve their own impediments not only get more valuable work done quicker, they feel greater satisfaction from it as well. They no longer feel helpless and a victim within an organisational bureaucracy but rather agents of change, creating the organisation that they feel is needed. As well as a greater sense of motivation, engagement and ownership within the team, there is also a benefit to the wider organisation of streamlined effectiveness allowing dedicated change agents or team coaches to spend more time on other aspects of organisational change.

RITUALS

Great teams tend to ask themselves "What can **we** do about this?" and focus on what is within their sphere of control while simultaneously looking to expand that sphere. Adding a question such as, "If we had more power than we assume we have, what would we do?" or "What is the worst that could actually happen if we went ahead and fixed this?" can be a great ritual to add whenever an impediment is noticed. Mapping out who else might be affected by what the team plan to do can help avoid local sub-optimisations or unintended consequences.

RESOURCES

Today we improved

THE SYSTEM

RISKS

Proactive improvement of the bigger picture is, in general, a sign of a very good team. However, there is a risk that the team acts outside of their sphere of understanding and unwittingly causes knock-on impacts elsewhere. The team may also be perceived to be acting "above their station" by going outside of their official remit which can lead to a loss of goodwill and even a drop in confidence should their attempts be shot down or seen to fail.

REWARDS

A team that is able and willing to think holistically is a great asset to an organisation. They no longer just concern themselves with "their bit" but rather look to make things better for the product, the customer and the organisation. Real solutions emerge and quickly. The team quickly gain confidence in their ability and a sense of fulfilment in their contribution to the organisation over-all. Exposure to parts of the process and the system outside of their normal interactions also increases their overall capability and thus agility as a whole.

RITUALS

To reduce the risks with this, great teams look to run small, safe, measurable experiments at first; with the ability to easily "roll back" to the previous state should anything go wrong. Drawing out a battle map, Mikado diagram and/or causal loop diagram can be useful to help the team consider affected parts of the system and how to safely address things. Also broadcasting intent before acting can help make unknown stakeholders aware of how the team's actions could impact them. Keeping the product's architecture as simple as possible through continuous refactoring is another helpful ritual here.

RESOURCES

Today we...
learned some
NEW SKILLS

We are now more resilient as a team because there are fewer SPOFs*

* Single Point Of Failure

#AchievementUnlocked

INSPECT AND ADAPT

Today we learned some

NEW SKILLS

RISKS

The main barrier to learning new skills is fear. Many people will fear going outside of their comfort zone to learn, practice and develop a new skill. They may well be unconsciously expecting to be judged personally for any professional failures as they develop new skills and may also be concerned that broadening their skillset will reduce their ability to develop their primary area of passion in greater depth.

REWARDS

Learning new skills helps to create T-shaped people and they are of much more value to an agile organisation. Because of this, individuals will see their marketability increase as they have multiple strings to their bow and allow a team, and therefore the organisation, to focus on the valuable work rather than the work our bottlenecked skills allow us to focus on. People will feel able to contribute more to the team and thus be part of more-successful deliveries. Rather than dilute their primary skillset, T-shaped individuals have a greater understanding of how their primary skill fits in to others.

RITUALS

Visualising contrasting futures can help individuals take the leap of becoming more T-shaped. Imagine a future where, in three years' time, you still only have one skill and compare that to a future where you have two or three different skills. Which one is a more attractive future for you? Using fear-setting to reduce and manage the fear associated with the journey is a helpful ritual while a practical "three amigos" style set-up allows teams to get into good habits of skill sharing.

RESOURCES

Today we we beat our

PERSONAL BEST

RISKS

It's rare to see too many downsides with a team continually striving to improve on their previous best, but whenever we start focusing on beating targets there is a risk of gaming the system or losing focus on the truly important things. Sergey Bubka broke the world record for men's pole vault thirty-five times because he received a bonus every time. It is debatable as to whether we – and the fans – truly saw the very best from him. Similarly, teams can focus too much on the numbers potentially at the expense of the delivery of value for the customer.

REWARDS

Beating our personal bests gives us a great feeling of accomplishment. Every team is different, operating with different skills and in different contexts and other teams in the organisation are not our competition, so focusing on competing with ourselves is healthier and keeps things within our control. Keeping an eye on what is going on elsewhere is useful because there are always things we can learn and, if another team manages to raise their bar, that can be inspiring to us, but great teams always focus on becoming the best they can be.

RITUALS

Great teams focus on fewer things simultaneously and dedicate time and attention to improving the things that are most important to them. Gathering data about your current "personal best" is essential to know whether you are improving and then regularly reviewing what has helped you get there and what could help you improve. Great teams always celebrate both achievement and effort too. Make sure you can view your targets, visualise achieving them and then verbalise your commitments to others.

RESOURCES

Today we immediately changed
OUR PROCESS

RISKS

The risks with making improvements on the fly is that they can have unintended consequences, sometimes ones that we don't notice straight away. In some cases our good intentions can actually end up making things a lot worse, for us and for other people or teams, so we do take care when making improvements. Autonomy can be a scary thing for everyone and mistakes will occur; these mistakes can crush the confidence of a team and the trust of leadership if a team does not have the skills and the space to learn.

REWARDS

Getting into a habit of fixing things as we see them can speed up our time to recovery and rapidly enhance not just the product but also the system and environment we are operating within. It increases our sense of autonomy as a team and our sense of empowerment, both of which help us grow into a great team. Procrastination often leads to costly delays and bureaucracy can creep in, which is a stifler of self-organising teams. A side-benefit of this approach is when we identify something and decide not to act straight away and see the issue resolve itself. We then become much better at deciding when and when not to act.

RITUALS

When an opportunity to improve is noticed, try getting into the habit of asking whether there is any need to wait before acting on it. A quick checklist of questions can help get the benefits while minimising the risks here. Questions such as "What could go wrong?", "Is there any need to act right now?", "How could I undo this if I needed to?", "Who should I tell?" and "How should I document what I am about to do?"

RESOURCES

Today we improved the

LITTLE THINGS

RISKS

By focusing on tiny improvements, we run the risk of ignoring the big changes that could make dramatic improvements; it is easier to push those important impediments to one side because we know we can make a little tweak here or there. Those little tweaks could end up being like "rearranging the deckchairs on the Titanic" – ultimately pointless because we haven't tackled the really important, big ticket items as a team. There is also a risk that we awaken our perfectionism trait by trying to achieve perfection when switching our attention to another area of improvement could lead to higher returns for our effort.

REWARDS

Small, regular improvements add up amazingly quickly and improving something that we are already good at is a positive starting point for teams as we are not starting from scratch. Getting just 1% better every day will lead to an improvement of 3,778% over the course of a year! And it's not just the improvements that are important, it's the habit and the culture that creates within the team and within the wider organisation. We become a learning team and a learning organisation; one that becomes accustomed to continual change. This helps us become resilient and less fearful of any change that may come our way while also providing an important factor of motivation for people within complex domains.

RITUALS

Tiny habits are easier to put into place than big changes to established behaviour. Starting with the smallest possible commitment you can think of increases the chances of a change being made and it's almost impossible to avoid over-delivering on that commitment. Attaching a new habit to an established one makes it easier to build into our routine and by verbalising the commitment we are more motivated to make it happen.

RESOURCES

Today we facilitated

OURSELVES

RISKS

If a team is forced to facilitate themselves, or they do not perceive they have the skills to facilitate themselves, then there is the risk that ceremonies do not happen. There is also the risk that an immature self-facilitating team will allow the dominant voices to run the show and freeze out the quieter members or converge too quickly on a prematurely identified solution. There is also less chance that the overall dynamics of the team will be noticed and reflected upon if there is no specific facilitator thus limiting the growth of the team.

REWARDS

A team that can effectively facilitate itself has less need for formal ceremonies as a lot of the work can be done "in the moment" or "ad hoc", improving team productivity. Facilitation by the team, for the team, is also often much more efficient and a sign to everyone that this team has great ownership, motivation and focus. Teams that can facilitate themselves also find it much easier to step up to removing their own impediments and have assertive conversations with stakeholders within the project and the organisation.

RITUALS

Great teams start small and begin with a ceremony such as a daily stand up or a "pre-planning" or "pre-review" meeting to build confidence before inviting in the extra dynamic of external players. Offering to facilitate another team's ceremony is also a good way to build up those facilitation muscles in a safer space than with our own direct colleagues. Great teams also ensure that the responsibility for facilitation is shared across those willing to do so and often in a paired format to increase safety and diversity.

RESOURCES

Today we stopped and

SWARMED

RISKS

For anyone looking in from the outside, the process of swarming – everyone stopping what they are doing and working on the same problem – can seem incredibly inefficient and chaotic. There is a risk that "too many cooks spoil the broth" and having too many people involved may slow down or over-complicate the solution. Also there is a risk that by just focusing on one piece of work we will delay other important work items.

REWARDS

Teams that make good use of swarming see tricky problems eliminated incredibly quickly and also to a much higher standard due to the collaborative nature of the problem solving. If we feel comfortable to call for the swarm, then we waste less time banging our heads against the metaphorical wall, struggling by ourselves. This also proves to everyone else that it is OK and beneficial to ask for help. By working on a problem together, we gain a collective and cohesive understanding of both the problem and potential solutions. We cannot help but share and learn about all of the skills and perspectives related to the problem at hand across the whole team and increasing our overall resilience as a team.

RITUALS

While many good teams will swarm when something goes wrong, great teams are more proactive about swarming and will plan in some time to tackle critical work items. If you use sprints or iterations then look for opportunities in your sprint planning where you could benefit from swarming. Some great teams will also experiment with specific "swarming days" or "swarming times". Also try to increase the diversity in your swarm (perhaps by inviting external stakeholders) so you can cover the full lifecycle and as many perspectives on the problem as possible.

RESOURCES

Today we
HIT BUG ZERO

RISKS

In order to eliminate bugs from the product, development needs to slow down so we must be prepared to take a short-term productivity hit. Secondly, actually hitting bug zero may not be a good thing because of the high cost of achieving perfection. We may end up slowing down too much or spending too much looking for and fixing things that only add marginal benefit. Great teams may collaboratively decide what a practical interpretation of "zero" is and aim for that.

REWARDS

The feeling of having something that works is amazing, and it speeds up our development massively. Not only that, but we can release with confidence, spend less time and energy on support and have happier customers and users. The habit of building something properly and fixing things immediately inevitably leads to higher quality and a greater sense of pride. Also, deciding whether it is cost effective to fix each bug encourages a more holistic, value-based decision-making process.

RITUALS

Collaborating on a definition of "zero" and then creating a clear, understandable process to categorising bugs will help tremendously here. Great teams don't argue about whether something is a bug or a change request, they work out together how to make the distinction then ruthlessly apply that protocol. Creating a visualisation of the known defects will allow teams to see their progress towards elimination and celebrating each success will increase and maintain motivation.

RESOURCES

Today we left the product in a

BETTER STATE

RISKS

Constantly looking to enhance things can tap into people's perfectionist tendencies. Great teams know that they don't need
a perfect solution but they do need an excellent solution. If we
focus relentlessly on enhancing the status quo, one thing that
will inevitably lose focus is new functionality. There is little point
having a small number of features working perfectly if we don't
have enough functionality for a working product.

REWARDS

Teams that proactively improve the quality of the product they
are building not only improve their ability to add functionality with confidence but also reduce the amount of manual
"fire-fighting" as a result of bug fixing. It is a happier, less-stress-
ful place to work and teams can afford to become more creative
as they are confident in the technical integrity of the product.

RITUALS

Pairing is a great way of getting into the habit of enhancing the
current status of things. With one person "driving" the work, the
"navigator" is able to have a wider field of vision, noticing the
irregularities on the periphery or in the wider context. Inviting an
external set of eyes is another good ritual because we tend to
see what we expect to see. Many great teams will employ the
"Boy Scout Rule" as part of their team charter and often proactively plan in time to enhance the product every iteration.

RESOURCES

Today we
DELAYED A RELEASE

─────── RISKS ───────

Delaying a release will obviously cause some frustration from management, customers and users, and this could lead to the team's relationships deteriorating. Not only this but it can be demoralising for the team to see their work stuck in limbo, not being released. Feedback is also going to be delayed because we are not testing the whole of the product development life-cycle. Until we get through the whole lifecycle, there could be some errors or feedback that we are missing out on.

─────── REWARDS ───────

By not releasing sub-standard increments, we are setting a high-quality bar, ensuring that our stakeholders know what to expect. Great teams take pride in their work and the product they are building, so reputation is important to them. By experiencing the pain of not being able to release, great teams respond by vowing to make sure it doesn't happen again. They appreciate not increasing the future support and bug fixing that would have come from releasing with a low-quality threshold, and will instead ensure they keep maximum time in future iterations for new functionality and increasing the complexity of future work.

─────── RITUALS ───────

Great teams will consciously ask themselves how confident they are in the potential of the impending release. Asking every member of the team to display their support explicitly will increase the consideration about this aspect, but great teams will be constantly testing this objectively as well. This can be with their own quality metrics or perhaps benchmarks from operations. One team I know would put their personal mobile numbers in the release if they were confident in the quality level; if not, they wouldn't release it!

─────── RESOURCES ───────

Today we...
took a stand for

QUALITY

WE DO THINGS RIGHT!

Nobody would really have noticed if we hadn't

..but it was important to us that we did it right

#DoItRight

Today we took a stand for

QUALITY

RISKS

Taking a stand for quality can be seen as anti-agile and antago-
nistic and, as such, can damage relationships within the organisation. Those looking for progress may well look at the team as
the blocker rather than a bastion of quality and it can give the
team the feeling that they have the right to indulge their perfectionism rather than deliver something that works and then
iterate on it based on feedback. Great teams do not avoid the
exceptional feat of overtime or heroic effort, but they know that
this is a one-off rather than something to be expected.

REWARDS

By taking a stand, not only are we going to reduce the risk of
compromising the integrity and reputation of the product and
the inevitable negative spiral of quality degradation, but we are
also going to start the conversation around what quality means
within the organisation. We will gain confidence as a standard
bearer for what is right, having a knock-on positive effect on sustainable working practices within the rest of the organisation. By
knowing that a sustainable pace is expected, we are much more
likely to go the extra mile when it is truly needed.

RITUALS

Regularly reviewing our working capacity in our planning sessions, daily reviews and retrospectives will help us gauge what
is achievable and what is not. Checking energy levels every day
and monitoring caffeine intake as well as what time emails are
being sent can be useful things to keep an eye on. Having a des-
ignated "sheriff" within the team on a rotating basis can help us
keep a watchful eye on our standards.

RESOURCES

Today we...
got our first

DELIGHTED USER

They loved: _____

It made us feel:

INSPECT AND ADAPT

Today we got our first
DELIGHTED USER

RISKS

The main risk associated with delighting a user is that the team indulge in gold-plating or over-engineering. They try too hard to make something perfect that they forget about what "good enough" is and could even end up building something that costs more than it will ever make in return. Also, by focusing on one user, or group of users, we can easily neglect other users and, given that dissatisfaction is more powerful than satisfaction, we will end up with a negative balance overall.

REWARDS

Happy users rarely tell other people about their experience. Happiness doesn't breed loyalty either. Only delight leads to positive word of mouth and sticking with the brand if things get tough. Customers are also lazy and change-averse, so if you are looking to entice people away from the competition then delighting them is your only real option, bar hoping your competitors screw up badly enough to drive them in your direction. Delight is both vicarious and infectious. We get pleasure from delighting others and this energy will pay off in our morale and work.

RITUALS

It may sound obvious, but asking is the number one ritual that great teams get into – and not just reactive but proactive questioning. Questions such as, "'What are you expecting?" and "What would amaze you?" Tools such as the Net Promotor Score are easy ways to institutionalise this and building some Kano analysis into requirements gathering is also a helpful habit to get into. For more retrospective feedback, techniques like the Perfection Game can help tweak things from a 9/10 to 10/10.

RESOURCES

Today we became perfectly
IMPERFECT

RISKS

Settling for less than perfect can be seen as an excuse to get sloppy and let standards slip. This can be a worry for management but also team members who see themselves as more of a perfectionist. People who have perfect handwriting and perfect punctuation and those that have a more laissez-faire approach to things can find it difficult to co-exist with one another, so be sure to clarify that we are still aiming for excellence, just not expecting perfection.

REWARDS

Letting go of perfection will allow for easier decisions, more experimental approaches and greater creativity. Teams will stop trying to "gold plate" their deliveries and will make it easier to get products to a working stage quicker thus allowing feedback at an earlier state. Often, in complex and unpredictable environments our users don't know what they want until they can see what they don't want and teams will need to run multiple parallel experiments to find the right result. A perfectly imperfect mindset will enable this and have a great side-benefit of being able to deliver at a faster pace without dropping quality.

RITUALS

While still aiming high – especially when it comes to delighting our customers – great teams consciously discuss the realistic level of "perfection". They create a commonly agreed (and regularly revisited) definition of "What's perfect for us?" and build an understanding of what "good enough" is into the "definition of done" too.

RESOURCES

Today we prepared for

THE WORST

———— RISKS ————

One risk we might think about here is the practice of "thinking negatively" and getting into a pessimistic mindset can be a detrimental thing. Indeed, finding out just how many risks there are and how unprepared we are for them can be incredibly unsettling and we may also find out that actually there is very little we can do to prepare for some scenarios which can be demotivating. Disaster preparation is costly in terms of time, money and energy, and it can also become repetitive.

———— REWARDS ————

Once a team implements a process of preparing for the worst, their ability to recover from the unpredictable increases dramatically, leading to confidence, not just within the team but within the stakeholders, customers and users. Prepared teams are much calmer when responding to incidents and stress levels are lower as a result. They may even not dread being on support now! An added benefit is that because we now know that we can cope better with incidents, we don't have to over-plan for things. We just plan for what we need to plan for.

———— RITUALS ————

Teams find setting aside a regular time on a regular day (every other Friday afternoon for example) to be very useful and an honest debrief afterwards is invaluable. Having clear roles that are deliberately rotated can be brilliant and writing up the experience is also a great habit to get into, one that can be carried into the real incident support process for the creation of future training scenarios. Finally, defining a benchmark for what "getting our patient stable" means for us can help stop us from over-delivering at the wrong time.

———— RESOURCES ————

Today we achieved
SINGLE PIECE FLOW

RISKS

Focusing on one thing at a time appears to be highly inefficient. Not everyone will be busy all of the time and many stakeholders may be asking why their piece of work is not being worked on. A team may end up delaying a lot of work in order to focus on one item and this can cause tension and stress within the organisation. In practice, many teams find that single-piece flow is a little too extreme and can find it reduces their overall efficiency and effectiveness.

REWARDS

The rewards associated with single-piece flow are numerous. Not only will we increase our chances of getting our higher priority items complete sooner but we will also uncover any issues or bottlenecks with our processes much more quickly. Teams will get that feeling of completion sooner and the collaboration required will lead to better, more cohesive solutions with less handoffs later on down the line. Teams will be more likely to enter a state of flow and develop repeatable patterns for increasing their overall throughput and capacity.

RITUALS

To begin with, setting aside a certain amount of time and proactively planning for swarming [See card QC1] will help teams understand what single-piece flow feels like. Other rituals that can help include setting "work in progress limits" and reducing the overall size of work packages. Ensuring that the team has all the skills necessary to get something done without any external dependencies will also make this milestone easier to achieve and institutionalise. Gathering data around things like cumulative flow and cycle time will help teams find their optimum and make a case to stakeholders who are wary of reducing batch size.

RESOURCES

Today we...
showed

BOUNCE BACK
Agility

We got knocked down

but didn't sulk about it

We got back up, dusted ourselves off and went again

#BounceBackAgility

Today we showed
BOUNCEBACKAGILITY

RISKS

When we were learning to walk we fell down many times, got many bruises and, at times, it probably felt demoralising, tiring and uninspiring. Developing bouncebackagility involves a similar process of being knocked down and learning how to get back up. This is a journey for a team and there will be times when the team questions their ability to keep going. There will be many opportunities for them to give up, for management to resume control and for the team to go back to being just another normal team.

REWARDS

Operating in a domain of huge unpredictability, complexity and volatility requires experimentation and a lot of inspecting and adapting. Being able to do that and not feel down when we hit inevitable bumps in the road is inspiring. Not only that but it reduces the need for bureaucracy and unnecessary planning because we know how to make failure safer and a richer learning experience. After a team develops its bouncebackagility, they will be one step closer to a point where they can actually come back stronger from failure. Just like a body developing antibodies – they can think about becoming anti-fragile.

RITUALS

First of all, it is important for a team to have the right mindset. Having a set of mantras that they repeat to themselves can really help as they adjust to this new way of evaluating our environment. Come up with some helpful statements, for example: "We either win or we learn", "Fall down nine times, get up ten", "We haven't failed, we just found some ways that weren't optimal" and repeat these regularly... repeat them regularly... repeat them regularly...

RESOURCES

Today we appreciated

EACH OTHER

RISKS

The sharing of appreciations carries very few risks because not much can go wrong with pointing out what your colleagues do well. The main thing I have seen in some cultures is a mild form of embarrassment about saying "thank you" or "well done" or "I appreciate what you did there". However, once someone begins and it becomes normal, it is surprising how quickly this activity can become a staple part of great teams' daily routines. The only other risk is the appreciation appearing too vague and disingenuous. Great teams do not fake their appreciation but do take time to really think about what others do for the benefit of the team.

REWARDS

Knowing what you are doing well allows you to consciously do more of it. Being recognised for your efforts and what you bring to the team is a huge motivator and gives an enormous sense of wellbeing while simultaneously creating a positive amplifier throughout the team. Team members are more willing to share knowledge and help each other in an environment like this. Calling out appreciations for those doing great work for the team is a more positive alternative to dealing with more selfish members of the team. Instead of focusing on their "negative" behaviours, we can instead highlight what good looks like and allow those people the option of following that lead.

RITUALS

Many teams will give out small cards with messages of appreciation on an ad-hoc basis; some prefer a highly visible "wall of appreciation" while others will prefer a "gratitude box".Some teams will add a question into their daily meetings along the lines of "Who did I appreciate yesterday?" and some will build this activity into their retrospective ritual.

RESOURCES

Today we met each other for

THE FIRST TIME

RISKS

Meeting new people can be scary. Will they be nice? Will they like me? Will it be awkward? Meeting in social situations can be awkward enough, but meeting in a work setting with forced informality can be physically uncomfortable. These meetings don't need to be completely formal and structured but neither do they need to be an unstructured free for all. Both extremes reduce the effectiveness and can actually have the opposite effect to that intended.

REWARDS

Putting a face to a name is a great way to build a relationship; and relationships are key to teamwork. Once we have a connection, we can begin to build empathy, trust and rapport. Then we can begin to think positively about our new team-mates and assume positive intent. We can also learn how we can be our best version of ourselves so as to be a great team-mate. With more teams being spread across the world and who may not ever meet physically, don't forget to make use of the ever-improving technology to help you meet each other – even if it's virtual. The investment in time and effort is almost always well worth it.

RITUALS

Finding out the core values of your team-mates is a good start. These can be incorporated into a team charter where everyone can understand our expectations of one another. Telling stories is a good way to learn about each other and making it fun and informal is helpful here. An added benefit of learning about each other is that the more we have in common with someone else, the more positive we feel about them and the more trust and respect we are willing to give them.

RESOURCES

Today we created
OUR IDENTITY

RISKS

The main risk with the process of creating an identity is the time, energy and patience required to include everyone to an extent that they are comfortable with the outcome. For the team identity to be meaningful, every member of the team must be happy with it and feel their views have been incorporated. Many teams attempt to make this identity perfect straight away when actually good enough is good enough because the team can evolve this over time.

REWARDS

A strong team identity makes it easier to manage ourselves and know what is expected of us and our colleagues. Knowing that we have agreed on shared values increases our bond and also enables us to trust one another more, increasing performance and reducing anxiety. A team that is united around a common identity is more likely to experience flow, will be more resilient to the inevitable challenges that they will face and will be more confident at experimenting with the trickier parts of team development such as failing, arguing and fessing up.

RITUALS

Asking "What kind of team do we want to be?" is a good way to start creating an identity but sometimes asking "What kind of team do we NOT want to be?" can be an easier question to start with. Great teams will regularly capture stories of when they have (and when they have NOT) exemplified the kind of team they are proud to be and use these to help to build and then evolve their team identity. Great teams will often create some tangible artefacts – from the work related – such as a team charter, to the more social such as team t-shirts and playlists.

RESOURCES

Today we found out something really

IMPORTANT

RISKS

Finding out about our team-mates involves vulnerability, sharing information that perhaps we never expected to share with our colleagues. This can be scary and if someone in the team betrays that trust then it can cause irrevocable damage to the team unit, so go slowly. When it comes to finding something out as a team, this often comes as a result of an undesirable event so ensure that whatever has happened does not get attached to a particular team member involved.

REWARDS

By focusing on what we learn, we give ourselves the opportunity to take something positive out of a challenge, avoid making mistakes twice and build resilience every time we hit a bump along the road to Team Mastery. As individuals, we like people we think are like us and finding out about what we have in common increases our bonds. If we feel more attached to our team-mates, not only will we go the 'extra mile' for each other but we will also give each other the benefit of the doubt when challenges occur.

RITUALS

When kicking off a new team, project, sprint or even a new day, why not ask yourselves: "What have we have learned recently?" When we notice feelings running high or low (because of tension or disappointment) be sure to ask yourself "What can we take from this as a team?" One great ritual is to create and maintain a team gratitude journal to keep track of what we are grateful for as a team. Alternatively run an emotional seismograph every sprint to get a sense of how everyone felt during the last period of work. Also revisit your team values every retrospective to check they evolve with you as a team.

RESOURCES

Today we
TRUSTED EACH OTHER

─── RISKS ───

The main risks with building trust is that someone inevitably has to go first. Building trust involves being vulnerable and dependent upon someone else - two states that don't come easily to many people. We are vulnerable and dependent because if the person we are trusting lets us down then we suffer. If we don't suffer then we didn't really need to trust them. In reality, we will only know whether we can trust each other when things get tough and that is hard to simulate.

─── REWARDS ───

A team that has high levels of trust will take on more challenges, they will stretch themselves further and will resort to assuming positive intent rather than sniping whenever something doesn't quite go to plan. Collaboration becomes possible when there is trust, without it the most we can hope for is cooperation. Trust enables commitment to one another which is deeper and more powerful than compliance. At the individual level to know that I am trusted is a special feeling and to know that I can trust others is hugely comforting and rewarding.

─── RITUALS ───

Trust is not a binary concept. There are different degrees of trust and we do not need to jump from zero to perfect in one leap. Teams can set small challenges that allow trust to build incrementally, steps that won't be catastrophic if we fail. This can begin with small personal favours that, once fulfilled, form the foundations for future trust to be built upon. Activities that enable us to humanise one another and understand our stories, values and hopes are great ways to build empathy, which is a stepping-stone to trust.

─── RESOURCES ───

Today we
ASKED FOR HELP

RISKS

The main risk associated with asking for help is the feeling of vulnerability. If the team are not in a safe space (or don't feel like they are) then the team may fear repercussions in terms of judgement, career progression or other sanctions. If a team asks for help (and is given it) too early then the feeling of empowerment and capability can be reduced and faith in that team's ability to proactively deliver can also be reduced.

REWARDS

The first main reward is the proof that it is OK to ask for help. Destroying the perception that asking for help is a sign of weakness is a powerful realisation not just for our team but for others within the organisation. Quite often the "help" that the team needs is a dependency that can be tackled systemically to optimise the overall delivery cycle. A team that asks for help and is given it increases that sense of being valued; it's great to know that someone has your back and is there to support you when you need it. The other benefit to consider here is the benefit that it gives the people who you are asking for help from. People love to be able to help, so give them the chance!

RITUALS

Great teams will create rituals to make it easier to ask for help without making a big show of it. Perhaps have a visual system, either a specific colour sticky-note on the board, a "bat signal" light in the team area or add a question to your daily meeting addressing any help that might be needed. Consider the wording of your request, from something as simple as changing the request from "Can I get your help?" to "Can I get your input?" or using a structure to help make the request more specific.

RESOURCES

Today we developed our own
LANGUAGE

—————— RISKS ——————

Anything that is specific to one group, by definition, excludes others and this can create a sense of isolation or resentment from those who are not part of those in the know. This is even more dangerous if that happens within the team and there is little more damaging to team spirit than separate sub-groups forming. Another dangerous part of this culture is the use of banter, which must be treated carefully for the potential of people over-stepping the mark.

—————— REWARDS ——————

All great teams take greater ownership of their environment, making it their own and language is a part of that. Not only does a common language make it much easier for teams to make faster progress, but it also strengthens the bonds within the group. Teams that can advance to a more informal way of communicating with one another have the potential to accelerate the feeling of togetherness to an even higher level again. Teams can also begin to introduce a healthy level of humour and banter when they understand each other and what their boundaries are.

—————— RITUALS ——————

Developing a common understanding takes time and conscious effort, so regular communication and reflection will help speed this along. Personality assessments can be a good conversation starter here, although results should not be taken too literally. Ensure that everyone on the team is aware when the team composition changes. Consider creating a team dictionary to begin with, especially for acronyms as this will make it easier to refer to things without having to look silly and ask. It will also make it easier to on-board new members in the future.

—————— RESOURCES ——————

Today we made

WORK FUN

RISKS

The main risk with having fun at work is the perception that we are not acting professionally or taking the important things seriously. This perception can increase a sense of scepticism in areas of the business with whom we may need to interact at a later date. It can also lead to a certain degree of complacency within the team, picking only work that looks like fun. So making work fun needs to be placed in the context of clear goals and standards.

REWARDS

It is said that "If you do what you love then you will never work a day in your life". Great teams find ways to enjoy what they do and find ways to make what they don't enjoy more tolerable. Work and play are not mutually exclusive and greater creativity, productivity and morale are excellent by-products of a more enjoyable way of working. Most teams operate on the principle of "when we are successful we will be happy" but what if it's the other way around? Indeed, great teams tend to operate on the principle of "when we are happy we have a better chance of being successful."

RITUALS

Focusing on the goal of the work and the constraints that have to be worked within frees up the team to consider different ways of solving a difficult problem. Coming up with multiple different options for solving a problem is a great ritual that makes work more fun. When using different personas to help consider a wide range of options, great teams instil a certain playfulness in their problem-solving approach. Questions such as "How would Homer Simpson approach this?" or "How would Wile.E.Coyote approach this?" can be great starting points for a team to enjoy themselves and their journey more, even if you are just having fun thinking about the problem.

RESOURCES

Today we put the

TEAM FIRST

RISKS

Attempting to achieve consensus as a team and hear everyone out can take a long time and there is also the risk that teams bypass this effort by avoiding difficult conversations so the boat isn't rocked. If this is the case then compromising is the most likely outcome and this result is something that nobody is really happy with. Such false compromises can lead to teams not being audacious and not airing their true opinions.

REWARDS

As the old adages go "There's no 'I' in team" but "You can't have awesome without 'me'" and great teams combine individualism with collectivism. In a great team, everyone gets to be themselves while feeling part of something bigger. As a result, teams that reach this milestone will have consciously traded off a small part of their self in return for a place in the team; this trade – as all good trades are – is mutually beneficial and everyone leaves stronger and better resourced than before.

RITUALS

Great teams argue as if they are right and listen as if they are wrong. They debate internally and agree externally. They realise that agreement is not binary and so test for levels of support. Great teams do not agree to anything that violates one member's values and will use a protocol (for example, DECIDE Cards or the Fist of Five) to help facilitate this. When things get tough, great teams refer to their team charter and remind themselves of what being part of this team is about.

RESOURCES

Today we welcomed a new

TEAM MEMBER

RISKS

Changing the composition of a team can be disrupting. The ways of working that have been built up and become second nature will not necessarily continue to work. The newcomer will need to learn how things get done and how to contribute to the team. This can slow things down and introduce conflict again, forcing the team to go back to basics. If people are insecure about their position in the team then competition and posturing can occur and, of course, adding more people to speed up delivery is often a dangerous myth.

REWARDS

Bringing in a new member can freshen things up, forcing teams to question how they do things as they accommodate and on-board the newcomer. If the team has become complacent then adding a new ingredient into the mix can be a powerful boost. A new member of the team can bring a new skill or trait that can push the team forward or provide a better balance, allowing them to become more agile and resilient as a team.

RITUALS

Any opportunity to take another look at the skills, values and ambitions of your team-mates should be welcomed and there is rarely a better time than when a new team member joins. Find out not just about the new person but about your existing colleagues. Run the Core Values exercise individually and as a team, then revisit your team charter and any other team agreements or artefacts such as a definition of done. It is often a good idea to assume that the newcomer does not understand the business context so revisiting the vision, the high-level goals and any acronyms would be beneficial.

RESOURCES

Today we...
gave some honest
FEEDBACK

You were very assertive yet respectful in our stakeholder meeting today

I feel proud to be your team-mate

Thank you

In today's planning meeting, you spoke for nine minutes. I got worried about our "equal air-time" working agreement

Fair point. Thanks. I'll keep that in mind next time

It feels great to be able to be open and honest with each other

#TellItLikeItIs

INSPECT AND ADAPT

Today we gave some honest

FEEDBACK

RISKS

Giving open and honest feedback can easily be overdone by being overly critical or even personal. It is easy to fall into many of the feedback traps and make it about the person rather than the behaviour or offer criticism that cannot be acted upon. Hiding behind the phrase "I'm just being honest" has at times led to irretrievable breakdowns in team dynamics. Feedback should also be consciously analysed before accepting and acting upon it and if this is not acknowledged then tension and frustration can grow quickly.

REWARDS

Teams find ways to improve if they are able to talk about their shortcomings and mistakes, and teams achieve greatness by being able to be honest with one another. A team that can tell it like it is, with love and care for their team-mates, is a great thing to be a part of. We see support, humility and a drive for improvement at both the individual and the team level that is not only great to be a part of but also inspiring to see for other teams within the organisation.

RITUALS

The three-question mantra of "Is it true? Is it helpful? Is it kind?" can be useful to structure and design feedback for team members. Models such as Action-Impact-Desired Behaviour, Non-Violent Communication or Situation-Behaviour-Impact can be helpful rituals to put in place as teams practice sharing open and honest feedback. Great teams also feedback ritually to keep the balance between assertiveness and respectfulness. Combining these rituals with some strong team values or a team charter can help a team to reap all the rewards of honest feedback.

RESOURCES

Today the quiet one

SPOKE

RISKS

Putting someone on the spot and forcing them to participate verbally when they are not comfortable to do so can increase stress, build resentment and reduce team effectiveness so care should be taken when attempting to bring people into a conversation. The other trap that teams fall into is assuming that we need equal air-time when actually all we need is equal OPPORTUNITY. Saying "I have nothing to add" is perfectly fine.

REWARDS

If everyone feels comfortable to talk openly in the team, then more open, honest and holistic conversations can be had and we can leverage the benefits of diversity. Too often a spark of genius can be missed because we weren't looking or listening for it. In general, the quiet person is doing a lot more listening so often has a lot more analysis and observation to share. A wise person once said, if you are talking you can only repeat what you already know, but if you listen you might learn something. So not only does the quiet person get to benefit from participating but the normally talkative people also get to benefit from learning while listening.

RITUALS

Getting people's voices in the room early, even if it is something as mundane as saying hello or what you had for breakfast today, increases the chance of them participating more later. Liberating structures such as 1-2-4-All also make it easier for less-extroverted types to participate while shifting up the media to, for example, more written structures as opposed to verbal can help. Consider asking that team member whether they would prefer to speak first, last or somewhere in between.

RESOURCES

Today we...

DID THE RIGHT THING

We resisted the temptation of the easy option and did the right thing

It would have been easy for us to: _____

But instead we:

It made us feel:

#TeamIntegrity

INSPECT AND ADAPT

Today we did
THE RIGHT THING

RISKS

Unfortunately there is no "universal right thing" and so there is a risk that what we believe is morally and ethically correct, others may not. The word "right" also has the risk of inferring moral superiority and judgement upon others which can lead to resentment. Taking a stand can also be seen as dogmatic or evangelical rather than pragmatic, and could lead to short-term consequences that could have a lasting impact.

REWARDS

A team that is prepared to do the right thing, not only has a warm feeling of having kept their integrity but will also act as a role model for others in the organisation. Many people don't feel confident to do what they know is right but are galvanised once they see somebody else do it, and we can see a surge of activism. Usually "doing the right thing" means avoiding the allure of short-termism for the benefits that will be accrued in the longer term. These longer-term benefits enable greater strategic growth and will avoid the costs of having to recover from the consequences made when avoiding the "right thing".

RITUALS

Make it so that the short cuts you know will be tempting require greater effort than the "right thing". Ensure, when you are making decisions, to be explicit about what choice you are making and why. Perhaps take it in turns to play the role of "conscience" within the team to ensure that perspective is always being heard. Build "nudges" into your workplace that make it easy to do the right thing with questions such as "Would I be able to morally explain this decision to a group of schoolchildren?" or "What decision would a future version of ourselves be grateful we made?"

RESOURCES

Today we

FAILED

RISKS

When learning to fail, a team and its members can feel vulnerable. This vulnerability can lead to stress, so creating a safe container for the team to try things within is important. It is also still important to carry out a risk assessment for experiments that the team is going to run and set the boundaries for experimentation so that any consequences can be contained. Failure should not be glorified and it is not an excuse for lack of discipline or rigour. Neither should a team go out intending to fail. Rather, they are looking to learn as much as possible, as quickly as possible.

REWARDS

A team that can experiment safely open themselves up to infinite learning possibilities. Not only do they give themselves the chance to find the "best" way to do something but they give themselves the chance to create a "new best" way. Owning our failures is essential for Team Mastery. High-performing teams do not blame fate or circumstance, or make excuses, and they ensure they learn from failure. Successful teams will also tell other people about their failures; perhaps they can help others to learn from their experiences and it might just make it more comfortable for them to fail as well.

RITUALS

Try setting aside time for one experiment every week for six weeks, run it with rigour and celebrate the learning as well as the results. Describe what the purpose of the experiment is, what you hope to learn from it, how you plan to maximise your learning and how you plan to mitigate the downsides. How will you create a "control" so as to isolate the variable that is causing the change?

RESOURCES

Today we had our first
ARGUMENT

RISKS

Arguments can lead to outright conflicts and emotional outbursts that, if not managed or facilitated well, can be very damaging. There is a risk that teams argue for the sake of it and enjoy playing "devil's advocate", which is usually a significant waste of time and energy. Without a sense of unity, some arguments may be used as an excuse to air personal grievances, which is not helpful and actually reduces a sense of teamwork.

REWARDS

A team that can debate healthily, challenge one another and entertain different perspectives without getting personal or taking things personally are definitely one step further along the journey towards Team Mastery. In weak or immature teams, people will keep their opinions to themselves rather than risk an argument. This may feel safe and easy but inevitably leads to resentment, passive-aggressive behaviours and poorer decisions. For true Team Mastery, conflicting views should be encouraged to the surface.

RITUALS

To begin with, teams will benefit from a structure or template for giving one another constructive criticism and challenging one another's ideas. Non-Violent Communication and explicit ground rules can help here and explicitly stating that it is the idea – not the person – that we are debating is a good habit to get into. "The Rule of 7" – where the team agrees to come up with at least six alternatives before analysing anything – is a ritual that can help develop the team's ability to have healthy arguments. Also, many great teams have made use of different hats to denote different roles to be played in a discussion; for example, "The Devil's Advocate", "The Inquisitor", "The Evangelist" and so on.

RESOURCES

Today we...

FESSED UP

Uh-oh!

We realised that we had made a MISTAKE

...but people appreciated our honesty

We also reduced the impact by

☐ Apologising

☐ Asking for help

☐ Focussing on priorities

☐ Buying flowers/beer/chocolates

☐ Putting plans in place to avoid it from happening again

#LearnedOurLimits

Today we

FESSED UP

RISKS

Deciding to confess to a mistake takes courage. Of course there is the risk of sanctions and so people will always be tempted to either ignore it and hope it goes away, blame it on someone else or make excuses. If nothing else, we all tend to leave it a little bit longer than we should before owning up but, in general, the earlier we confess the better. Inevitably there is a risk that people will lose confidence in us, the process and the product, so it is no excuse to just be haphazard in our decisions in the knowledge we can just say sorry and everything will be ok.

REWARDS

One immediate benefit of admitting a mistake is the crystallisation of the consequences. These consequences often turn out to be nowhere near as bad as we thought. This makes it easier to try things again in the future. Admitting when something goes wrong also has the benefit of increasing trust because we know people aren't going to lie to us and they are also less likely to fail again in the future. If there is a status issue then admitting mistakes can make other people feel safer as you are no longer seen as perfect.

RITUALS

The failure bow is one habit that teams can experiment with to make it easier to admit and learn from failure. When we know failure might be a likely option, framing our actions as experiments or hypotheses can make it easier to acknowledge a "less than optimal result". Regular check-ins also make it easier to let people know that something isn't going well. The longer we leave it, the harder it becomes to put our hand up.

RESOURCES

Today we didn't ask

PERMISSION

RISKS

Teams that just act without asking do get more done quicker but there is a risk that they make bad decisions that have unintended consequences. It is more likely that a team will de-risk decisions less effectively and perhaps repeat past mistakes that they could have learned from had they asked. Deliberately doing something that they know they would not be allowed to do can also cause tension in a relationship and decrease trust, making it harder to gain permission for other ideas in the future.

REWARDS

Getting permission can be time-consuming, whereas if we know the result is likely to be positive, it is far more effective to just get on with it. A recent Standish report concludes that reducing decision latency can improve your project performance by 25% [1]. This greater autonomy that comes from not asking permission is valuable for team confidence and self-management. Also, if we are looking to encourage autonomy within our organisation then one team acting on their own initiative can be a great example for others to follow.

RITUALS

A simple and quick de-risking process is a wonderful ritual here. Try fear-setting or just asking a few questions such as "What could go wrong?", "Who could be negatively affected by this?", "How could we make this decision safer?" and "How could we roll back if we needed to?" can really help the team make more rounded decisions before going off-piste without necessarily going through the full permission process.

[1] https://books.google.co.ukbooks?id=WV1QDwAAQBAJ

RESOURCES

Today we challenged
THE STATUS QUO

RISKS

Things are as they are for a reason, and it may be that we just don't appreciate the reason behind the status quo. People are also loss averse, so the prospect of a new status quo that involves them losing their current view of the world will risk unsettling people and may put them on the defensive. If there is no perceived solid argument for change then people may view the change as disruptive and may even take it as a personal challenge rather than a challenge to the process, structure or overall culture.

REWARDS

To cope, and indeed thrive, in a complex domain, teams and organisations need to be constantly inspecting and adapting both what we do, why we do it and how we do it. As well as helping remove obsolete, inefficient or ineffective working practices, we will see more empowerment, engagement and motivation and, as such, the resilience and continued coherence of the wider organisation will be enhanced. Change is the new constant and there should be no "sacred cows" when it comes to processes or structures; everything is up for tweaking, pivoting or adapting.

RITUALS

Taking time out to "hack the system" on a regular basis can be a good way to get into a habit of evaluating the relevance of what we do. Constantly asking "Why do we do this?" or "Why do we not do that?" is another helpful ritual while mapping out processes, structures and workflows can help visualise what is going on, making it easier to spot opportunities for improvement. To be balanced, great teams also try and understand the value that may be being accrued from things existing as they currently are.

RESOURCES

Today we...
got really

CREATIVE

Not just a different font!

...I mean a completely Original way to do something

*It was scary / cool / surprising / _____ *Delete as appropriate

satisfying / energising / _____

#AgileImagination

Today we got
CREATIVE

RISKS

The main risks with creativity lie in people's perceptions about their ability to be creative. Many people doubt their ability to be creative and also fear the results of their efforts being judged negatively. That fear then escalates to a personal fear of being judged foolish so a safe environment is a must. We must all suspend our desire to critique, analyse and judge ideas until the creative idea generation process has finished. If ideas are judged before then, it will inhibit people from putting their ideas forward.

REWARDS

While teams value rhythm and stability, they hate monotony and enjoy the opportunity to try things without fear. Not only will the product and the organisation receive more innovative ideas but a team that exercises its creative muscles more, tends to get greater fulfilment from their work. The process of opening creative channels also increases the chances of engaging more members of the team, which has to be a good thing.

RITUALS

Try setting some constraints in your idea generation process, such as coming up with seven ideas before deciding on one of them. The hat of creativity can also be added to any meeting to encourage one person to indulge their innovative energy. Changing the environment – for example, a room with a high ceiling and natural light – is another ritual that teams have used to stimulate greater creativity. Other helpful rituals are to think of 100 uses of an everyday object, use story cubes to make a story or find a random image then brainstorm captions for it. To get into a creative mindset, try playing an improv game.

RESOURCES

Today we...
considered

MULTIPLE OPTIONS

before deciding what to do

Sure it was uncomfortable and at times we felt we were going around in circles

but we ended up with a richer decision as a result

#ConsideredChoices

INSPECT AND ADAPT

Today we considered
MULTIPLE OPTIONS

RISKS

If there is a clear solution that is definitely good enough then deliberately taking time out to consider other ways of doing something can be wasteful. If the decision-maker has already firmed up a solution in their mind then those involved will feel that their effort in considering other options is going to be wasted as everyone knows what the decision will end up being. Also, because people in general prefer certainty, engaging in divergent thinking can lead to anxiety.

REWARDS

By opening ourselves to multiple possibilities other than what we are used to, there is a chance that we come up with a radically new and better way of doing something. If there are no good practices to follow, then creating and running multiple parallel (and safe to fail) experiments is the best way to deal with complexity and may even help us realise we are addressing the wrong problem to begin with. Teams that get good at considering multiple options are not only more innovative, but also encourage greater participation from everyone within the team.

RITUALS

Set-Based Design and Design Thinking allow us to limit the impact of our cognitive biases by exploring the problem space through randomisation and/or empathising with our customer. Questions such as, "If we had absolutely no constraints, what would we do?" or "What would Batman do?" can help, as can creating a constraint such as "No decision can be made until we have at least seven options". Increase psychological safety by deferring judgement of ideas and allow a period of silent idea generation to encourage full participation.

RESOURCES

Today we integrated
EVERYTHING

RISKS

Stopping the various strands of work and integrating them all together takes time and is something we will often try and defer until we have got things "perfect". Integration is painful but is a necessary activity to get something that is actually valuable and usable. Agile teams will need to do this sooner and more regularly than they would like, and this can affect morale in the early days of team formation. Integration will also feel like it is slowing us down but if what we are doing will ultimately not work then the speed we are working at is false anyway.

REWARDS

As well as the motivating factor of seeing everything come together, making our true, integrated progress visible helps build trust and confidence in our customers and other stakeholders. The earlier we find the issues with integration, the sooner we can work to make this process smooth and painless, and the more we repeat it, the less of an issue it becomes. It builds confidence in our release and operations processes and allows us to get a real feel for our pace of delivery. Other rewards include greater resilience and courage to share our status as well as confidence to seek more regular feedback by involving our customer and stakeholders.

RITUALS

Teams will typically make use of iterations as natural points in time to bring everything together. They will often also push themselves to demonstrate something tangible and "end to end" so they and other stakeholders can get full visibility of the status of the work. Great teams will work tirelessly to get to a point where this integration happens automatically and continuously so that whenever any changes are made, we are notified immediately if anything isn't working as expected.

RESOURCES

Today we
MET OUR FORECAST

RISKS

If there is too much focus on the numbers then a team may simply reduce their forecast to increase their chances of meeting it. If there is an expectation for the team to increase their forecast next time then more games can be played, such as deliberately inflating estimates. Teams who are too concerned with meeting forecasts may also scale back their experimentation and innovation simply to focus on the numbers.

REWARDS

In a complex and unpredictable environment, getting to a level of predictability is an anxiety-reducing feeling for everyone. When a team understand their capabilities and work well enough to be able to predict their capacity, it becomes a lot easier to manage expectations both within and outside the team. Great teams who understand their capacity benefit from being able to develop a sustainable pace over the long term, reducing any pressure to compromise quality and introduce technical debt.

RITUALS

Benchmarking to previous iterations is a key ritual for teams when attempting to establish their predictability. Gathering data on when the team under-forecast and over-forecast will allow them to inspect and adapt based on empirical evidence. They will be able to notice patterns and put in place as many positive patterns as possible. One of these patterns is usually associated with the size of work items. The smaller the work items, the more predictable the work and, therefore, the forecasting becomes.

RESOURCES

Today we got stuff
"DONE DONE"

RISKS

Getting "done done" is often an impossible challenge for many teams because of the length of the true value stream and the limited extent of the cross-functionality of the team. This can lead to teams feeling helpless when working towards this milestone, so this may be a card utilised many times as a team takes incremental steps towards "done done". Some team members will be anxious about the prospect of what is needed of them as individuals to help achieve this – becoming more T-shaped for example – and may unconsciously resist this change.

REWARDS

The biggest reward for getting "done done" is the realisation of actual value for our users. We also get to test assumptions and find the bottlenecks in our process as soon as we get end-to-end delivery. These things can be hidden if our definition of "done" is limited to "delivering to the next part of the process". As well as bottom line and quality benefits, there are huge benefits to morale within the team as they get a sense of true completion and closure. Team members who become more T-shaped will be more able to deliver real value and will also become more marketable into the bargain.

RITUALS

Mapping out the full workflow and setting a regular challenge to extend the definition of done every iteration will help a team get there much quicker. Challenging our assumptions about what is possible and finding mutual benefit for everyone involved in the necessary organisational and structural changes to extend our definition of done will only help increase our progress towards this milestone.

RESOURCES

Today we cut

A DEPENDENCY

RISKS

Cutting dependencies often involves bringing that piece of work into the control of the team or removing a piece of the workflow that we have found to be unnecessary. The risk with bringing more responsibilities under the control of the team is that it is harder to complete that more comprehensive piece of work within the timebox. Another risk with removing a part of the workflow is that we make a mistake or build a workaround simply to remove a dependency and end up reducing quality or safeguards.

REWARDS

By reducing dependencies, we become more able to be truly agile. We are able to get things "done done" as a team rather than handing off to the dependency or having to wait. Things get done quicker and we learn to look at the bigger picture rather than just our small piece of it. We feel a bigger sense of completion and like we are truly adding real value while also reducing waste and the overall time to deliver. Our ability to spot bottlenecks and quality issues increases because everything remains within our line of sight, so defects will drop.

RITUALS

Mapping out and visualising the workflow and highlighting the dependencies using string and/or coloured sticky notes is a great start here, then asking ourselves to consider reorganising team composition to reduce the dependencies. In the short-term, simply following the work and observing how the dependency is resolved currently can provide great insight into how to tackle it permanently.

RESOURCES

Today we reorganised to

DELIVER

RISKS

Reorganising a team is very disruptive as it requires re-forming the identity of the team, developing new relationships, building up trust, and re-creating a sense of capacity as a new team. We may lose the delivery ability of the current team and there is no guarantee that the new set-up will prove to be more effective; it is a gamble. Not everyone will want to try something new or feel safe enough to leave their area of specialism, so there is a risk that this upsets people.

REWARDS

Being able to reorganise gives us much greater ability to deliver value as a team, a highly motivating factor for all great teams. It increases our resilience at a team level as we know that we can flex our roles to what the work requires of us. Each individual within the team will also get exposed to more skills and opportunities, increasing their ability to contribute to the delivery and extend their skillset – making them more valuable both within the company and outside.

RITUALS

Great teams will regularly evaluate their definition of done and this time point is a perfect opportunity to look at the skills within the team. Another natural point to look at reorganisation is at the end of a release, where the following release may require different team capabilities. Reorganising mid-release can be very disruptive, so finding a natural point where the value outweighs the disruption is key to success. Another way to ease gently into this more fluid and flexible way of working is to experiment with pairing or even "The Three Amigos" [1].

[1] https://www.agilealliance.org/glossary/three-amigos/

RESOURCES

Today we mapped our

WORKFLOW

RISKS

Mapping out the whole workflow can be quite a time-consuming process for teams that have little visibility or understanding of how things work in the organisation or how their work fits into the bigger picture. It can also be demoralising for the team if the results of the exercise show how much of the overall process is outside of their scope of control and how daunting it seems to influence it.

REWARDS

Teams that can create this picture, or even just begin to create it, can benefit greatly from the increased visibility and wider awareness it brings. Understanding the full lifecycle gives the team an understanding of the potential consequences of any local actions, allowing them to think holistically and at a system level. It can build empathy with those neighbouring stakeholders and help spark conversations and even collaboration with them. Visualising clearly where the work is flowing – and where it is not – helps the team understand what "done" means for them and how they can go about extending it over time. Teams with a greater alignment are not only more productive and positive but also more able to highlight to leadership which aspects of the environment are helping and hindering their ability to create value at pace.

RITUALS

Great teams regularly revisit their process in their retrospectives and planning sessions when they consider the extent of their definition of done and what they are capable of committing to as a team. Every couple of weeks, great teams ask themselves how they can extend their scope of control and reduce the overall cycle time of delivery. Value Stream Mapping and Causal Loop Diagrams as well as Cumulative Flow Diagrams are effective tools for teams to making this visualisation easier.

RESOURCES

Today we
GOT RHYTHM

RISKS

Monotony can be a motivation killer for many people and in many cases efforts to establish a rhythm in an inevitably changing environment can prove futile. Also, aiming to achieve consistency can lead to forecasts being manipulated to increase the chances of meeting them rather than reaching an organic, natural level of predictability. At worst, teams may even avoid delivering extra in order to stick to their rhythm of previous deliveries.

REWARDS

The primary benefit of becoming more predictable is that the individuals both within and outside the team will feel lower levels of anxiety. Human beings feel more anxious whenever they are in a state of uncertainty and so being able to understand – with confidence – what they are capable of within a given timebox can be very reassuring. This predictability also helps anxious stakeholders manage their expectations and, in time, leads to fewer interruptions asking for progress updates because they can simply look at the data. Teams are more likely to enter the state of flow when they are operating at a predictable pace.

RITUALS

Abstract estimating is a good ritual for many teams to help them get away from dysfunctions around time-based estimation. Shorter timeboxes reduce the variability of forecasts and offer more data points for teams to work with and analyse, and limiting the amount of work on the go also increases a team's ability to get greater predictability in their work. Another good ritual is to break work items down into a consistent size as this is one more variable that can be kept constant.

RESOURCES

Today we got into

FLOW

RISKS

The greatest risk with getting into "flow" is that of gold-plating. Teams can lose track of time and end up over-delivering on a feature when that time could have been better spent elsewhere. The other risk is that the team becomes too delivery-focussed and loses its ability to indulge in creative thought and divergent thinking, which is an equally important mode for great teams to operate in.

REWARDS

It is often said that a great team is worth more than the sum of its parts. There is a similar compound effect when a team is in "flow". Not only does more work get done – and done better – but fulfilment increases and knowledge and learning sticks more than when the same work is done but the team is not "in the zone". Great teams learn how to balance deep focus with almost whimsical, unbounded creativity. Flow is the absolute manifestation of focus and great teams discover ways to capture this often-elusive state on an almost repeatable basis.

RITUALS

Each team that achieves flow tends to find their own common patterns that increase the chances of getting there. As a result, the most important ritual here is to reflect on the times when the team reaches flow and analyse the variables for commonalities. One very common factor across almost all great teams, however, is that of undisturbed focus. Whether it is going off-site for an afternoon, or a team agreement to turn devices and notifications off for three hours every week, every team I know that has achieved Mastery in this aspect of their teamwork has instilled some kind of ritual around undisturbed work.

RESOURCES

Today we

FOUND OUR WHY

RISKS

The main risks here are that the team spend too long getting involved in the business decision driving the work. It is ultimately not their job to decide what to build, for whom or for what strategic objective and focusing too much on this can distract from the actual work of delivery. There is also a risk that they begin attempting to change the problem being solved by applying their domain knowledge and perceptual filters or perhaps they disengage altogether because of a lack of empathy with the "why" behind the work.

REWARDS

A team that understands the problem being solved is more bought into seeing that problem solved. They can humanise the work as something that will help real people and they may even be able to offer suggestions for novel and technically creative solutions rather than relying on how business or the market currently sees the default way of meeting the market need. The main reward here is motivation as understanding why something is being done taps into both their autonomy and purpose drivers as well as helping them maintain resilience when the project goes through any tough times.

RITUALS

The easiest ritual to apply here is to regularly ask "Why are we doing this?" Clarifying the vision behind the work is a quick and easy way to help people understand what the effort is all about. A simple **Elevator Statement** or **Pixar Pitch** can work wonders here. This can filter right down to the micro level where user stories help engage teams in solving problems rather than being fed solutions to implement.

RESOURCES

Today we
OVER-DELIVERED

RISKS

The biggest risk with taking on extra work is that we will over-commit and end up compromising either the quality of our work or our mental or physical wellbeing. A team that is eager to please or that feels compelled to do extra can get themselves, the product and the organisation into a tough situation. Once they have set a precedent, it is then very difficult to revert to their actual speed of delivery as expectations will have been raised. Not only that, but the team is likely to be operating at lower levels of energy and motivation and from a position of lower quality.

REWARDS

A team that is able to figure out a way to safely improve their productivity will not only have a huge boost to morale but will also increase the satisfaction of their stakeholders. They should also be able to ritualise some of the enhancements to their ways of working for continued benefits into the future and these benefits could also help and inspire other teams within the organisation. This team will soon be feeling unbeatable and great teams also get a taste for continually beating their "personal bests". The sense of positivity will become infectious and will often also lead to greater creativity and innovation.

RITUALS

As counter-intuitive as it may sound, most great teams tend to consciously slow down so they can work out how to speed up; they give themselves the opportunity to improve their processes every time they commit to work. Great teams study their energy levels to plan in the most optimal way for them. Great teams also tend to have a motivational ritual to the completion of work – from banging a gong to ritually destroying the card representing that work item.

RESOURCES

Today we...

Today we...

Today we...

Today we...